D0430546

# TEENS DEALING WITH DEATH

Stories from My Students

SUSAN ROMERO

Copyright © 2014 Susan Romero
All rights reserved.
ISBN: 1500724432
ISBN 13: 9781500724436

# DEDICATION

To my students, past and present,
Who have experienced the death of a loved one…
this is for you.
May these true stories bring you peace
in knowing that you are not alone in your suffering.

CONCORDIA UNIVERSITY LIBRARY
PORTLAND, OREGON 97211

"Wouldn't it be great to have one volume where the personal, unvarnished feelings of bereaved adolescents were authentically expressed?   With a sensitive, experienced teacher sharing loving advice with each teenager as well as discerning counsel to the parents?   Then you must read Susan Romero's treasure trove of profound discernment of entering the world of the young person with invaluable support."

RABBI DR. EARL A. GROLLMAN
AUTHOR, *STRAIGHT TALK ABOUT DEATH FOR TEENAGERS*

# TABLE OF CONTENTS

# ACKNOWLEDGMENTS

THANK YOU TO the courageous students who
shared their story with the world.
You are changing lives for the better.

To Shannon, I remember when you were suffering through your
father's death some thirty years ago. I appreciate your willingness
to share your story. Your wisdom is invaluable.

A very special *thank you* to my very dear friend and spiritual mentor, Dr. Christina Grant. You opened my eyes to spirituality, and
for that, I am eternally grateful.

And a final thank you to my beloved father, you are my rock and
I thank you for your unconditional love and consistent support.

# FOREWORD

MY FACE HIT the asphalt before my hands could stop the fall. Through a tunnel I heard, "Are you okay? Are you okay?" As my conscious awareness returned I was helped to a sitting position where the first thing I saw was someone's sandaled feet. Following these feet upward to a face, I met the calm gaze of Susan Romero, author of this book.

In the week before I met Susan, death knocked on my door. It didn't ask for me, though. It summoned my best college friend with whom I shared an apartment. And not only her. It took another close friend too. Both were young, vibrant, funny, full of life, and suddenly gone. Life had just gotten real and I was unprepared.

On that morning 24 years ago when I met Susan Romero, we had arrived at an empty elementary school, new teachers-in-training. The students hadn't returned yet, but it was our first week of the teaching credential program and we were on site bright and early. During our first break one morning, I wasn't feeling well so I headed outside for air. That is when I blacked out.

The deaths of my two friends had overwhelmed me. I considered quitting the teaching program, but there had been effort, time, and money at stake. So, the following day I showed up, lip and black eye cut and swollen, pride and ego crushed, along with the heavy knowledge that death had come for people I loved.

It is in this context I met and became friends with Susan Romero. If I hadn't returned to class that following day, I would have missed getting to know the woman with the sandaled feet. We had a similar way of evaluating circumstances, of recognizing the ridiculous, and her sense of humor never failed to send me into much-needed laughter.

One of the notable talents I saw early in Susan was her ability to connect with kids who needed someone to respect. While some students ran teachers ragged and took advantage of every opportunity to defy authority, Susan's students respected her. She was able to work with kids from challenging backgrounds in any age group, and she had a quality in this regard that many teachers didn't have. I soon learned she had a particular skill for connecting to the adolescent. With their changing hormones, insecurities, attitudes of indifference, awkward stages, unique angst, and their desire for companionship, love, acceptance, and understanding, Susan had the knack.

Observing this about her and seeing from the start that she had innate gifts with young people, I know she is the ideal person to bring *Teens Dealing with Death* to the forefront. She knows her student population well. Her knowledge exceeds how they behave or how they're doing in class. She's gone to a deeper level and allowed her students an avenue to share their painful stories so an important message can be relayed, not only to other young people, but to us all: You are not alone. Loss is a human experience, and we're in this together.

*Teens Dealing with Death—Stories from My Students* brings awareness to the grief of teenagers. What does a teenager do with grief after losing a key figure in their life? By bringing greater awareness to the plight of these teens, they can be guided to continue their journeys—not fractured—but in wholeness.

We have a difficult time with grieving in our culture. There is a push to return to "happy" as soon as possible. Thus, we have developed a model of repression where grief is buried. But if the grief doesn't have an appropriate outlet, feelings of aloneness and isolation can intensify. This is especially true for teens, who are too young for the harsh realities of life and unsure how to proceed when faced with them. Holding their grief inside, this private pain pierces them deeply.

Enter the young, brave voices in this book and their teacher Susan Romero, who have taken a courageous step to break the silence by sharing their eye-opening stories of the death of a loved one. These young people, no longer children but not yet adults, openly talk about their losses and discover in the process that they aren't alone, that quite a number of their peers have suffered as well.

These precious souls faced the painful death of someone close to them at a very sensitive age. They have taken the first step in healing: sharing their thoughts and feelings with us. They didn't sugar coat their stories, as we're so fond of doing in polite society, but rather laid out the bare truth. In doing so, we come to a better understanding of their experiences, confusion, loneliness, mixed emotions, and above all, their amazing resilience.

The many voices in this book have each felt a cutting harshness at an age when ideally they would be spared such a thing. But, the truth is that mothers can be taken from us in childhood. Fathers can be stripped from us just when we need them most. A grandparent we've relied on to sustain and support us can suddenly be gone. A brother we thought we'd share our entire life with can die leaving us to wonder why. What is this about? Why did this happen to me? What will life be like? How do I live now?

*Teens Dealing with Death—Stories from My Students* opens the door and welcomes you inside where you're met by other young people who already have been initiated into the world of loss. Ultimately, author Susan Romero asks, "How can we approach teens and the subject of death with more reverence? How can we treat death with the sacredness it deserves, rather than something to avoid and quickly move beyond?" She suggests we begin by being aware of the desire to escape or avoid the inevitable. We must give the dying and their loved ones the gift of having our full presence with them, not in fear and anguish, but with compassion.

We are not taught to bear witness to the suffering of those we love, or to be in the presence of death with a soft heart. Because there are few examples, we must learn to do this on our own. When we are presented with the honor of being with a grieving teen, we can do it with a soft heart. We can be fully present in the atmosphere of death, to be a steady support for a teen experiencing the rawness of their first deep loss.

*Teens Dealing with Death—Stories from My Student*s reveals the heartbreak that happens when a teenager loses a loved one. We learn in these pages that many adults aren't sure how to handle these situations. Susan Romero shows us how to be present in the face of grief. It's what she has done with her students for over two decades, and she now shows us how to more skillfully connect with teens so we, too, can help them find peace.

Christina Grant, PhD
Author of The Holistic Approach to Breast Cancer—
Every Woman's Guide to Health, Vitality, & Wellbeing

―――

"The very fact that God has placed a certain soul in our way is a sign that God wants us to do something for him or her. It is not chance; it has been planned by God. We are bound by conscience to help him or her."

Mother Teresa, *The Joy in Loving: A Guide to Daily Living*

―――

# 1

# SENT TO ME FROM SPIRIT

TEACHING.

In my opinion, it is single handedly the most rewarding job that one can have. To make an impact on young people's lives goes far beyond the curriculum. It goes deep into their heart and soul. I have been blessed to work with young people since 1991, and I consider it my calling.

My eighth grade class was different this year. I had a wide range of rascals and as the year progressed, I learned that I had more than a normal amount of students who had suffered extreme loss during their short lifetime. Grading an essay, I would learn of a death, and then in a speech, I would hear of another. In conversation at lunch, yet another student would share with me the death of a beloved parent. It was heart wrenching. It is noteworthy to mention that as an educator who teaches in a middle class neighborhood that I occasionally have one or two students yearly who have suffered the death of a parent or significant being in their life. So, as I started to realize the alarming number of students affected, I was moved to take an informal poll.

As each class wrapped up, I asked gently, "How many of you have lost a parent or a parent-like figure in your life?"

I saw hesitation at first. Their little eyeballs told me who my people were as they glanced left and right around the room. I said that they could tell me in private, and I shared that I was discovering quite a number of students who had experienced the same thing in all my classes. Hands slowly inched up, as many as four in two separate periods. I noticed a sense of relief wash over them as they realized that they were not alone in their loss. What started out to them as embarrassing and awkward, ended up becoming a group that they weren't afraid to be a part of. An odd sense of pride was exhibited. They found peace in knowing that others in their class had gone through the same pain and that they were not the *only* one.

As seventh period rolled around, I was shocked at the total number of students that I had discovered. I also learned in this process that many had lost siblings, grandparents in the role of the sole parent, and best friends.

That was when I had, as Oprah would say, "a light bulb moment." This moment came when I determined that I had fifteen students who had suffered a terrible loss. I was in awe of such a number. I'd had no idea. There must be a reason that so many were placed in my classroom.

Louise Hay, founder of Hay House and a wonderful soul whose essence has transformed millions of lives, has said, "When God calls us, we need to answer." Well, the number of my students affected by death was unprecedented! I was being called. I felt these students needed to tell their story, not only to help them heal but to bring this issue into the open and to help others deal with it.

The next day I asked my affected students, "How many of you would have liked to have read something written by teens that had already lost a parent or significant loved one? How many of you think that having read something like this would have helped you deal with their death?"

Unanimously, they all agreed that reading stories about other teens in similar circumstances would have helped them. Many of them to this day have not read anything on death and dying. They simply buried their loss.

I began to search. I found that there wasn't much available for teens. There were picture books explaining death for young children, self-help books for adults, but it was limited for teens. That had to change. This book is the beginning of that change.

God works in mysterious ways. These children were placed in my classroom. In education, it is common to find out something tragic about one of your students, but it's rare to learn about something of this magnitude affecting so many.

My "aha moment" was this writing project as a means of healing for my writers as well as for their readers. Death happens on a daily basis, and I'm finding that as a norm we aren't dealing with it. I'm hopeful this book will help teens worldwide that are about to lose a loved one or ones that have already suffered a tremendous loss.

Not all of my students participated in writing their "chapter" of the book. In a few cases, the surviving mom or dad said no to my student's desire to participate. One wasn't ready. Two didn't want their "dirty laundry" aired out for the world to see. I understood that. Another declined because they were battling the same issues that took the other parent. That being said—the stories in *Teens Dealing With Death* are willingly told by my students. They wanted to help other young teens know that they are not alone. They wrote to share their heartbreak in hopes that readers will identify with an aspect of their story and that the pain of losing a loved one at a young age may be lessened by knowing that many of us have gone through similar losses.

After each student's chapter, I write a personal letter to my student in hopes of easing his or her pain. I provide insight on what I feel may specifically help them based upon my interactions and observations of them on a regular basis. My students are still hurting and instinctively I had to help. As a result, transformation occurred. Through conversation and expressing themselves, I noticed and felt the change in my students. We were on to something.

The following excerpt is from a student who wished to remain anonymous for private reasons. This is the student who shared his loss with me during a lunchtime conversation, and it was this conversation that gave me the notion that his story and stories like his would be of benefit to others who suffer in silence.

Life can be a good thing or a bad thing sometimes. Stuff happens that you don't want, and it makes you feel like you're stuck in a deep, dark hole that you can't get out of. Well, that's what happened to me.

When I was five, my life started to change because of a thing called cancer. It took away my mom, my sister, and my niece. They were a great inspiration in my life. They helped me through life, especially hard times. When they died, I felt like my life was over.

I still had family. My grandma and her mom were there for me and tried helping me get out of the hole. But when I was ten, my grandma died in a car accident. Her death was another downfall in my life. She was one of the most heavenly beings you can imagine: so nice, so sweet, and so kind. It was like she was my God, but since she died, I started to do drugs and bad stuff. The pain was intolerable.

My other granny, thank goodness, slapped me into reality. She showed me love, passion, and care, and then four years later she died from old age. I didn't know what to do then—die or still hang in there.

Right now, I choose to hang in there, to live with this feeling of being stuck in an endless hole.

⸻

IT IS MY belief that there are no coincidences in life and that everything happens for a reason. I believe spirit brought my kids together. I paid attention. The kids agreed to share, and here are their stories. It is our hope that you identify with something in their stories and that they bring you a renewed sense of peace.

# 2

## LOST TWO IN ONE

I'M ACQUIELLE, AN African-American fourteen-year-old girl from
Modesto, California. I have spent the majority of my life floating
between Arizona and California, and I currently live in a foster
home with my twelve-year-old brother. I am a straight A student
who enjoys playing basketball and reading books. I write my story
because my daddy was murdered on June 12, 2012.

My father Dominic was a forty-two-year-old people person—
a loving, generous, and caring man. If he had it and you needed it,
it was yours. My father loved to cook, and he shared his cooking
skills with the entire neighborhood. Fried chicken was his specialty.

Everyone who knew my father was well aware that he loved
his family deeply, especially his children. Dominic had eleven children, and I was his 8th child.

He was always happy, and he would chase one adventure after
another. My dad was open-minded, active, funny, and fun. He
would take us regularly to carnivals and state fairs. Around the
house he would play basketball with us, and he was a real good
dancer; he was best at popping. He was always wrestling with the
kids, and it wouldn't be uncommon to see me walking on his back.

He was very protective over his family, and he would guard his family with his life.

My dad was very smart, and whenever he walked into a room, he brightened it up. It was hard not to love my father. My daddy made me feel safe and happy all the time. His smile put me at ease and in his presence, I felt that nothing was wrong. All was good in the world, and I miss him so much!

I remember it like it was yesterday. When it happened, I was 13-years-old and my brother was eleven. We were in our rooms, and I was reading *The Fire Within* when my aunt called us into the living room. Whenever we were called into the living room like that, we were in trouble. Due to her tone, I thought we had done something wrong. We went in looking scared, and I sat down on the end of our tan couch and my brother sat right next to me.

I asked, "Are we in trouble?"

"No," my aunt responded very sadly. She looked like she was about to cry. Her eyes were watery, and I feared the worst. My mind went to everything that could have happened; my heart was in slow motion as I waited to hear what she had to say.

"What's wrong?" asked my brother in a questioning voice. By the way that he looked at her, I could tell my brother was worried about my auntie.

"Well... your dad was walking with your uncle when someone shot him and...he died," she said in a sad, serious voice.

Never in my mind did I think that she was going to tell me that my daddy was gone forever.

When I heard her say those words I couldn't believe it! I was shocked. Someone knocked all the wind out of me. It took a while for me to digest what I just heard. My brother sat still and said nothing. I ran to my room and cried my heart out into my pillow for hours. I was thinking I'm never going to see him again. How could that be? He was indestructible. It wasn't possible for him to be gone. I thought about how my life was going change. I just cried and cried until I couldn't cry anymore, and I didn't talk to anyone for the rest of the day. I felt safest in my room and wanted to be left alone.

My aunt finally came into my room and that's where I learned that he had died at the hospital. She told me stories about how she and my daddy grew up together. Stories about when they were young. She told me those things to make me feel better, and it worked. It felt good to hear stories about him. The weeks following his death she continued to bring up my dad and tell me all about him. Since he couldn't tell me himself, she made sure I knew who my father was.

The last time I spoke to my dad he told me that he loved me, thank goodness. That was on my brother's birthday, May 31st, two weeks before his death. Sadly, I didn't get to see my daddy a lot as he lived in Stockton, thirty minutes away. He drank a lot, and he hung around trouble; the police even knew him by name.

It's been one year since he passed away, and it still feels like a piece of my heart is missing without my father. I really thought I would be miserable for the rest of my life. For a long time, I had that feeling that my heart was dropped down into my stomach. I actually thought about killing myself a couple of times because it was so hard to process such a loss. I couldn't take the pain anymore. My biological mother was no longer in my life, and now I had no one.

The funeral was in Fresno, California, because dad's father was buried in Fresno. (My grandfather died before I was born.) So, my auntie, my brother, and I drove from Sierra Vista, Arizona, to California, and on the way we picked up my sister in Pasadena, California.

First came the viewing. This is where you can visit the body the day before the funeral. There was a strong scent of flowers inside the church. That smell of flowers is glued to my brain, so whenever I smell those kinds of flowers I think of seeing my dad in his coffin.

The church had seven rows of seats on both sides. Right down the center of the aisle sat my dad's light-blue coffin. When I walked to my dad, and saw him in that coffin I cried a lot because I just couldn't believe he was gone. His lifeless body just lay there in that coffin.

He didn't look like the man that was my daddy. He didn't look the same at all. He was yellowish and he looked swollen, kind of rubbery. It's very difficult to describe. It just wasn't HIM. Clearly, his soul and spirit had moved on. I was just hoping it was all a dream, that when I would wake up the next morning, he would be sitting in the living room watching TV. If only....

For my dad's funeral all the Fresno family came. The funeral home was like four times bigger than the church we went to for the viewing. My dad looked very peaceful in his coffin. I didn't cry as much that day because I accepted the fact that he was gone. There was nothing I could do about it, and I was just thankful for the time we had together.

I sat in the front row with my sisters, brothers, and mom. Yes, my biological mother came to the funeral. My biological mother reminisced to my cousins about the times she had with my dad. She cried a lot. My brother sat silent during the funeral. In fact, he hasn't really ever talked about it. To this day, my brother has held his pain inside and as a result, he has some anger issues.

The funeral began with an opening prayer, and the scriptures Psalms 34:3-8 and 1st John 3:14-15 were read. After that, we did the words of expressions and my cousin read a special poem from my dad's funeral packet. I particularly liked his special poem to the point that whenever I hear it, I cry. Finally, the pastor read the eulogy and the final prayer. The last thing we did was the burial of my father, and the song "Amazing Grace" played as he was lowered into the ground. I was thankful my mother was also at the funeral so I didn't feel so alone.

You may be wondering why I didn't leave with my mother after my father's death and why I'm in foster care. My Auntie was considered my Foster parent at the time and there would have to be court to attend and paperwork drawn, so I stayed with my Auntie. Unfortunately, I'm not with my Auntie anymore. My Auntie couldn't afford to keep us anymore. She wasn't receiving any money from the system because she was a blood relative and the strain on her financially to take two more children in was too much. So, I am now in a foster home with my brother.

My birth mother has not started the paperwork to get us back and has officially lost her rights to us. It's like a 1% chance that we can be together again. That's what I've been told by my social worker. I miss my family. I miss having a mom. I miss having blood relatives to spend holidays with. I miss being like everyone else.

Here is what I am thankful for. I am thankful that I still have my brother to share my life with. I'm thankful for my wonderful foster mom. I am thankful to share my story with you to help others realize that they are not alone. I was dealt a tough hand in life, and I'm a survivor.

Since his passing, my dad has appeared twice in my dreams. The first time was on his birthday, July 22nd. In the dream we were coming back from the bakery and once we walked through the gate, my dad came in behind us. When I turned around and I saw him, I paused because I was in shock. I ran up to him and gave him a giant hug. We went for a walk and he apologized to me about everything he put us through. I cried tears of joy. I was so happy. I actually woke up crying. That was one of the happiest moments of my life.

In my second dream, my dad and I relived all the times we had together after my mom and dad split up. The part I particularly remember was when my sister was coming to stay with us. My daddy, my brother, and I were at a hotel so we could pick her up and take her home with us. When my dad left to get my sister, I took a nap in my dream. When he came back, he woke me up, and my sister was standing at the doorway smiling. I was so happy to see my beloved sister because I hadn't seen her for two to three years. I woke up before I could finish that dream. Experiencing this dream made me feel a little more complete, like he wasn't really gone.

To remember him on his birthday, we always write a note to him in sharpie pen, tie it to a helium-filled balloon, and send them up into the sky.

If I knew my dad was going to cross over when he did, I would've been around my dad and talked to him as much as possible. I would also try to talk some sense into him and help him as much as possible. He had a serious drinking problem where he couldn't go a day without a drink. It would make him feel sick and weak to not be intoxicated. He didn't have a job, so he, my brother, and I would have to ask for money, and when we got some, he would use up a lot of the money on alcohol. Yes, that makes me sad. If there had been someone more persistent in helping him to stop, he might still be alive this day. I would love to tell him how much I love him.

If I could give advice to someone having to go through this, I would tell him or her a couple of things. If they are in a situation like mine, I would recommend that they help their parent as much as they can to lead a good life. That way the death may be prevented or the one dying can pass away happy and leave good memories for the living to remember. I would also let them know even though they're gone, just how much their lost loved one still loves and cares for him or her.

I would like to share this poem because it was read at my dad's funeral and it helped me accept the fact that he was gone:

I'm Free
Don't grieve for me, for now I'm free.
I'm following the path God laid for me.
I took his hand when I heard him call,
I turned my back and left it all.

I could not stay another day.
To laugh, to love, to work, or play.
Task left undone must stay that way.
I've found that place at the close of the day.

If my parting has left a void,
Then fill it with remembered joy.
A friendship shared, a laugh, a kiss,
Ah yes, these things I too will miss.
Be not burdened with times of sorrow:
I wish you the sunshine of tomorrow.
My life's been full; I've savored much,
Good times, good friends, a loved one's touch.

Perhaps my time seemed all too brief,
Don't lengthen it now with undue grief.
Lift up your heart and share with me,
God wanted me now; He set me free.

My mom calls me on a regular basis nowadays. It started about two months ago. She tells us how much she loves us, how much she misses us, and what is happening in her life. She's planning to visit my brother and me soon. We will see if she keeps her word. We can only hope.

In closing, those of you that are losing a parent or have lost one, remember my story and know that however awful you are feeling, you are not alone.

This is a letter that I hope my dad will get to read someday:

*Dear Father,*

*I love you! I miss you so much, and I hope you're having the time of your life! I want you to know that I'll never forget about you, and you'll never be replaced in my heart.*

*I will do anything for you, and I know you did everything you could for us. You protected us in your life, and I am so thankful that we had you for as long as we did.*

*Thank you for everything you did for us... I love you!*
*With Love,*
*Your daughter Acquielle <3*

—※—

*My dearest Acquielle,*
*I must first tell you how brave you are for your willingness to share your story. My heart aches for all that you've been through. You are such a*

beautiful soul that is hurting so much, and please don't doubt that there isn't anything that I wouldn't do to help and to try and heal that open wound. When I think of you in the long-term, this is what comes to my mind. Please listen clearly so that you are able to have the next chapter of your life be rewarding and filled with LOVE.

As you move forward in life, Sweetheart, don't be afraid to let love in. My fear for you is that you will be afraid to let someone love you for fear that they may also walk away from you or be taken from you. That you may be so afraid subconsciously of experiencing that again that you won't let anyone close to your heart. Please don't let that happen.

The tricky part is that you won't even realize that you are doing it. So, always keep this wish of mine in the back of your mind so that when you do find that special someone, you give him a key to your heart. Don't hold back as scary as it might seem. "'Tis better to have loved and lost, than never to have loved at all." (footnote Alfred Tennyson, In Memoriam)

God/Spirit/Source/whomever you believe runs the show has made your life experiences thus far a part of your life to help you learn something about yourself. Yes, it sucks, but that's what life is all about.

Lessons.

Whether it's to show you how immensely strong you are or to show you and the world your incredible courage, or to simply show you the errors of your parents' ways, please know that you have the control here. It may seem like your life is out of your control, but in reality, it has thrust you into the driver's seat.

Don't repeat patterns of behavior that you know lead to lifestyles that aren't good for you. Learn from their mistakes and make a better life for yourself. I love this quote from Mother Teresa, and it made me think of you, young lady. "I know God won't give me anything I can't handle. I just wish he didn't trust me so much."

He trusts you a lot, girlfriend, and knows that you will pull through this.

Let love in, Acquielle. Let love in. From The Perks of Being a Wallflower, "We accept the love we think we deserve."

*You deserve the MOST, Acquielle, the MOST! Yes... you ARE that AMAZING!*

*I'm so sorry for your loss. I love you.*

*~Ms. Romero*

# 3

# IT WAS A SECRET

I'M TONNY, A fifteen-year-old heading into the ninth grade. I am a Cambodian-American whose mother was born in Cambodia. I have four brothers and two sisters, and I am the middle child. I was born in Fresno, California, and moved to Modesto in the first grade. I've been living with my grandma since then.

Despite what's happened to me in my life, I'm quite normal. In 4th through 7th grade I was a 4.0 student, and this last year my GPA was a 3.8. I think Victoria Justice is super hot, and I love to play basketball even though I'm 5'2 with mad skills. I was even a member of my school's basketball team. I watch sports and play video games everyday when I'm not playing basketball.

I consider myself to have a lot of friends, and when I grow up, I would love to go into business, engineering, or the technology fields. Despite all this, I lost my wonderful mother when I was five-years-old.

Toun was my mother's name. She had curly, black hair with light skin and hazel eyes, which is unusual for Cambodians. She always wore Cambodian-style clothing. She was married

Cambodian style in the United States to my father, but it was not an official American marriage.

My mother was always cleaning from what I remember. Not sure if she enjoyed it, but it's what she was always doing. I loved that she was strong and took care of the entire family while my dad was away gambling.

I especially remember my time with her when she and I would sit home, snuggling and watching movies. She hugged a lot, and I sure loved my hugs. She always told me to do my best in life. Unfortunately, my sweet mother died of organ failure due to drinking and smoking at around thirty years of age.

My mom didn't tell me that she was sick, but the rest of my older family members knew. Looking back now, she kept on getting skinnier. I never thought that I would lose my mom so early; I didn't even really understand death.

My actual last memory of her was walking through our old neighborhood in Fresno with her holding my hand. I sure miss her.

When she died, I had to find out by myself because nobody wanted to tell me. I was told she was on vacation. I was six when I actually found out that she had passed away.

I was at my grandma's old house, which was also in Fresno, California. I was hiding around the corner listening to my aunt talk about my mom's funeral. Standing there, I couldn't believe my ears. WHAT? What was I hearing? Instantly, I was overwhelmed with sadness and so angry that no one had told me.

Knowing my mom died, I felt like the other half of me was gone. My heart was split in two. The emptiness in my stomach made me sick. What was even worse about her loss was that I found out by myself.

It gets even more complicated. I felt completely alone because I couldn't tell anybody that I knew the truth because they didn't want us to know. I would have gotten in big trouble for eaves-dropping. We weren't supposed to know that my aunt was going to become the "mom" to my younger siblings. They didn't want to tell my baby brother that his mom really wasn't his mother, and my younger brother actually still doesn't know. My aunt is his "mother" now that my mother is no longer with us.

With me knowing the truth, it posed a risk that the younger siblings would find out. I didn't handle this discovery well because all I did for two months was cry. Now that I think of it years later, I guess crying was better than holding it all in.

When I was around eleven, my brother started talking to me about my mom. My older brother told me that he was the only one allowed to go into the hospital room to see her because we were too young to be let in.

He said that my mom tried to get out of her hospital bed to say goodbye to us, but the doctors put her back in bed and wouldn't let her leave. I was never able to say goodbye.

To be honest, I can't tell you how the funeral was because I wasn't there. My dad didn't let my siblings or me go to the funeral. My aunt tried to take us to the funeral site, but the cops arrived before we could even get out of the car. I only got to see the front of the building at the funeral, that's how quickly the police showed up.

Apparently, my dad didn't know that we had left for the funeral, so he called the cops when he noticed we were gone. My dad wasn't at the funeral either; he was at home. My dad had a restraining order against my aunt. The order was to keep her from him and from us because she stabbed him right above his hip after she found out about my dad's affair with my mother's best friend. He had cheated on my mom with her best friend before she died. Can you imagine the blow to my mother's heart?

I suppose it was this betrayal that killed my mother's spirit, and her organs followed with it. I heard that my aunt also stabbed him because he wouldn't let me see my mom when she was dying. Obviously, she got arrested for this, but she is out now. This is only one reason why I don't like my dad, another reason being that he didn't let us attend our mother's funeral. I don't hate him though.

As for visits, my mom has returned to me in a dream. All I saw in the dream was my mom and I holding hands in my old neighborhood walking down the street. I was a younger Tonny in the dream, and she was wearing a white shirt and a white skirt. We just walked together, hand and hand, no words spoken–just a happy feeling inside.

To me, the dream meant to always be thankful for the memories I shared with her. When I woke up, I felt like I had just seen a ghost. Thanks to this process, I became more open in my thinking, and my mom was able to manifest herself in one of my dreams.

When I was seven, I heard a song that seemed odd, much more than a mere coincidence. The song was "I'll Be Missing You" by P. Diddy. Without reason, I felt like I was about to cry when I heard this amazing song. This song is about somebody remembering someone that has passed away and missing him or her a lot. I will never forget the first moment that I heard the song, and it was the following lyrics that hit home with me.

I will always be missing you,
While you stare at us from heaven.

I immediately thought of my mom. My mom is definitely missed, and I will always love her.

One time when I was eleven, I was missing her, and I thought I felt my phone vibrate in my pocket. I took it out of my pocket and my mom's picture was on the screen. The picture was in my photo gallery, but it popped up on my screen randomly. I felt bittersweet emotions, happy cause she was right there with me, but boy, did I miss her.

My family does rituals for her every year on Chinese New Years. We pray for her all day at a temple. We also put food out for her, so that she has a wonderful meal in Heaven. Also on her birthday, my family and I go to the cemetery and say happy birthday to her. Her ashes are buried in a mausoleum in downtown Modesto.

I think it would have helped me mentally if my family actually told me themselves that my mom had died. Also, I think it would have helped if I hadn't known that my dad had cheated on my mom. My brother was the one who told me that. I was only ten-years-old when I heard that. I felt like I was about to throw up. I'm sorry that my mom had to go through that.

My brother, Kevin, who is twenty-two has really been there for me about all of this. I'm glad that he has been open with me. Since he was older when mom died, he knew her more and I'm sure her loss hurt him more. I understand how this led him toward making bad choices. He participated in a drive-by shooting and was in prison for five years for it. He's doing a lot better now, and he just got a job recently. So, I am happy for him.

As for my dad, I haven't seen him since my mother passed away. We don't talk either. My older brother and I are the only ones who live with my grandmother. My younger siblings live with another one of my mom's sisters. So essentially the family broke up after her death, and I lost a dad then too.

I wish I had changed my level of communication with my family after I found out the truth. If I had told my family about how I felt, I think it would have helped me. I was sad. I knew the truth, and they didn't know I knew.

I would have also changed my involvement. I would have snuck out of my house and gone to my mom's funeral anyway. I feel like I missed out on an important life event because I was afraid to react and disappoint. I'm so sorry, Mom.

To anyone suffering from the loss of a parent, it's okay to tell your family or your close friends about it or how you feel. Don't be ashamed to cry, and never forget the memories you had with them. It will get easier, but it will never go away. So… be strong, you aren't alone.

---

Dear Mom,

If you can hear me, I have so many things to tell you. Even if we didn't have that much time together, I think you're the greatest mom in the world. I wish we did have more time to spend with each other, but I know that you're always watching over me in Heaven. You are the most beautiful and strongest woman in the world. You raised seven kids on your own, and I'm so proud of you for doing that. We came out so great because of you. I wish I actually went to your funeral that day, instead of being with my horrible dad. I love you so much, and I just wanted to tell you that. I loved the days we spent with each other. I will always remember the memories we had with each other. I cried for months after I found out you passed. I felt like my other half disappeared.

Again, you are the strongest woman in the world, and I love you so much.

Love,
Your Son Tonny

---

Dear Jonny,

You are absolutely precious inside and out! So glad you were placed in my classroom. Your smiling face behind those super chic reading glasses on a daily basis was so appreciated. You are such a kind, loving soul.

I can't imagine how it must have felt to be that little boy hiding around the corner and learning of your mother's death! I can visualize you, and my heart aches for that little boy and the young man you are becoming.

Know that it happened that way and there is nothing you could have done to change the behavior of others. It is also not a reflection of you. You were just a child, and it is no fault of your own. When this happens in life, it's important to acknowledge the mistakes and make sure that you don't repeat mistakes made by others. Learn from those mistakes...and sometimes that takes forgiveness. They thought they were doing the right thing. It's unfortunate that they underestimated your sheer brilliance and keen awareness. Your resilience is admirable.

Keep smiling, Tone-Loc, you are a wonderful human being.

As for your mommy, she is with you, and this saying from a headstone in Ireland is fitting for your story. "Death leaves a heartache no one can heal, love leaves a memory no one can steal."

No one can take away those memories, my dear.

Love you dearly,
Ms. Romero :)

# 4

# WAS I TO BLAME?

I'M VERONICA AN 8th grader who is an only child and was born and raised in Modesto, California. I am also a Girl Scout in the Cadet Troop, #3402. In my spare time, I hang out with my friends and family and enjoy swimming. In school, I am a straight A student, and I play string bass and violin for the school orchestra. At home, I love the TV show *Friends*, and my mom loves it too. After watching one episode of it with her, I was hooked. My favorite character is Rachel. We aren't alike, but her character cracks me up. I also love to travel and have been to Mexico, Oregon, Nevada, Virginia, District of Columbia, and of course, all over California.

My dad Paul was born and raised in Long Beach, California. He worked in the computer software programming business in the Bay Area, and he was very good at his job. He collected a book of awards for developing solutions to eliminating big viruses in computer systems. He loved his job. In his free time, my dad loved to challenge his brain a lot, and he loved solving puzzles. Wednesday nights were always Poker Nights, and he would always partake in that. He loved his time with friends. As a teenager, he played football and had a good arm. He was a very funny man with a great sense of humor. I always hear about his sense of humor and as a girl, I always remember laughing around him. Everyone says I have my dad's sense of humor, as well as his curly hair. I was his only child, and he had just turned 38 when he passed away.

I was seven and a half-years-old when my daddy died suddenly from leukemia. It happened quickly. He suffered a headache that day, and we truly didn't know the severity of the situation.

I was home alone with him on January 20, 2008. My mom went to the store to buy my dad some Advil since he had been complaining of his head hurting. He was in his bedroom, and I was watching *Parent Trap* in our living room. When the movie ended, I checked on my dad cause he didn't come out of his room for the entire length of the movie.

I found my daddy in his praying position. He was kneeling on the ground with his hands in the prayer position. There was blood on the sheets. He apparently had a seizure when he was praying and had bitten his tongue. I think I walked in on him during the seizure. He started vomiting, and I could see his body retracting/ heaving. I went into the corner, outside the room by the door because I was afraid, and I didn't want to see him get sick. I looked over again, and he vomited three more times.

I ran to my bathroom and started screaming, "Daddy, Daddy, Daddy!"

He would always come running when I would do that so I was hoping he would come to me. He didn't come.

I got up, and I went back to the end of the hallway where the room was. He was still in the prayer position, his head resting on his hands.

All I can remember is that I stood there in shock. I just stood there. I didn't want to leave him. He seemed awake, but he just couldn't respond. About ten minutes passed, and my mom arrived.

I ran to her and said, "Daddy is vomiting!"

She ran to the room, and he wouldn't wake up. He wasn't responsive. So she grabbed a bucket of water and tried splashing him, but he wouldn't wake up. Then 911 was called. She called her mom and then my dad's parents. At that moment, I really didn't know what was going on. My mom took me out to the living room. I was numb. I had no idea what was happening. I was focusing on my cat at the time because she would always want to go out and for some reason she didn't want to.

When the ambulance arrived, they took him on the gurney to the hospital. I knew he was off to the hospital, and I wondered what was going to happen next and when would he be back. I didn't know what was wrong with him. He was in his underwear, and I knew something was wrong cause he would never go out in his underwear. He looked peaceful and in no pain. The seizure looked painful, but he appeared to be resting.

What happened to my dad, you might wonder? It turned out to be a fast growing tumor in his brain. They knew twelve hours beforehand that we were losing him. I personally didn't know this, but the adults in my family did. They didn't want to tell me to protect me from hurting, I imagine. I knew that he went to the hospital because he was sick. You never think death. Someone is sick; they go to the hospital; they get better; and they come home. That was my thinking.

When I found out he was gone, I was at my Grandma's Paulette's house (my mom's mom). My mom was crying, and my grandma was comforting her. I asked, "Does this have something to do with daddy?"

She hurried to the bathroom and got sick, and my grandma followed her. I really didn't think anything like my dad had died. I thought she was just "sick."

Mom returned crying, her face looked freshly wiped. Her breathing was erratic. The kind of breathing that you have when you have been severely crying, and you're trying to catch your breath. She took a real big breath in and said, "Daddy's dead."

What?

Of course at first, I didn't think it was true. I started crying, and they both comforted me. I continued crying.

From there, we went to my dad's mom's house (my other grandma). I got a lot of attention that night since none of the other cousins were there. I was the only kid there, and being the only kid there was nice.

I remember putting on a show to make everyone feel better. For example, I performed acts surrounding the seasons. For Christmas season, I pretended to get shocked by the lights. I just tried to make everyone laugh, and it kind of worked. I felt really comforted at my dad's parent's house, and I felt everything was okay because the family was together. It felt like my dad was there, and everything was okay like any other holiday. It was easy to forget why we were together that night. Since everyone else was there, it was easy to imagine that he must have been there too.

My mind kept playing games with me. I thought that my dad's death wasn't real. Then reality would set in. Then I would flip flop back to it's not real, and then I would realize that it was.

Sometimes, I would think, "Oh, we are waiting for him. He'll come through the door any minute." I would think he would be coming back, and then I realized that he wasn't because he actually died. It's so hard to explain how I came to terms with it.

When I finally got it and realized that he had actually died and that he wasn't coming back, I felt out of breath, weightless, and I couldn't stop crying. I was not hungry at all, and I couldn't really eat. I was in shock and completely devastated.

As for a goodbye, he was unconscious for those twelve hours so I was unable to really say goodbye. I was in the waiting room of the hospital, and he was hooked up to tubes. My mom didn't want me to see my dad like that. I know that I may not have wanted that last image of my dad all hooked up to tubes and unconscious, so I understand my mom's decision.

At the hospital, my mom brought in a photo box with an audio clip from when I was three-years-old. It was a gift box for my dad, and it had my old picture inside it from when I was a little girl. She brought it into the room with her. There, my dad went into cardiac arrest where the heart stops, and the nursing staff brought him back to life with the defibrillators, the electrical pads that shock you back to life. He came back to life. Then, my mom played the audio message from me to him in my voice from three years old: "I love you, Da-da." It was then that he passed away for the final time. I think he actually came back to life to hear it, and then he was ready to move on.

"I love you, da-da." He heard my final words even though I wasn't there to say it. That gives me peace.

As for his funeral, I attended, but I didn't really participate. I was mostly with my Grandma Paulette at the funeral. Looking back, I wish that I would have. I wish I could have honored him and done something. At the funeral, I didn't believe it at first, but then I cried non-stop. I tried to stop crying. In my mind, I wanted to be strong for my mother. I know it pained her to see me upset, so I put on a strong face. Then I would realize it again, and it hurt. The reality of losing my daddy just hurt so much.

Since my daddy passed away, he has visited me in a dream. I was a seventh grader and twelve-years-old when he came to visit me. In the dream, I was at a hotel. Everyone I knew was there, and I got separated from my group when I heard my dad's voice in the lobby of the hotel. The first thing I heard was his laughter. I stopped. Looking in that direction, I saw him there laughing. I walked toward him, and then he noticed me. He started walking towards me too. It was like he wasn't dead. I was so excited to see him, and he was really happy to see me.

He said, "You're really grown up now."

I was wearing a long nightshirt in the dream, and what's the first thing I do? I explain to him why I was wearing that cause I didn't want him to think badly of me. I wasn't dressed for a hotel lobby; I was in my pajamas. Ahhh!

Seeing him brought me so much relief, and I was really happy, smiling from ear to ear. It was so weird...it's hard to explain. I was in the hotel. He was standing there in my dream, admiring me. He also said, "I've missed you. How are you so old?"

Then, I told him that I really missed him too.

Then I woke up on the couch thinking, "WHOA... that was awesome. I finally had a dream with him! He came to me in a dream!"

I was so excited. I told my mom and my Grandma Paulette immediately. They looked surprised and thought it was cool.

Since then, I think about my dad all the time, and whenever I see bright orange old school cars, it reminds me of my dad. Orange was his favorite color; he loved orange! Old American Graffiti style cars are rarely seen, especially in the color orange, so when I see one I think of him, and it makes me smile. At first, I didn't notice them and then my mom said, "Hey, do think that's a sign from your dad?"

I actually do. It's an old car symbolizing something from our past, and it's orange, his favorite color, on top of that!

Soon after he died, I wrote him a note and put it on his gravesite. To this day, we continue to visit him there. We decorate his gravesite every birthday and for ALL holidays. He especially loved Halloween. One Christmas, we decorated it with lights, flowers, and balloons. For his birthday, we bring balloons and sometimes we bring proof of my accomplishments, such as certificates from school. His gravestone has Superman imprinted on it because he loved superheroes. My dad was our superhero.

I've experienced another death in my family since my dad passed away. My cousin Kayla who was a year younger than me, died exactly the same way my dad did with leukemia (35.1%), but she was able to survive a year. She was 8. It's just weird that it was the same kind.

If I could give anyone any advice when it comes to losing a parent, the pain from the loss comes in waves. It is also okay to cry and to be angry. It is also okay to ask questions. Be a part of the funeral. Pay tribute to them. I just wish I could have. I would feel more at ease if I had paid tribute to him. A public goodbye of some sort; show the world how much I loved him. My daddy knew how much I loved him, so there was nothing left unsaid between us. But, please make sure your loved one knows how you feel because you just never know when your last moment with them will be.

—∞—

Dear Daddy,

I really miss you, no hard feelings on how you left. I'm not disappointed that you left so quickly. It really wasn't your fault.

I know I haven't been open to messages from you much, but I am open now for messages. So, message away; I'm ready. I also have to say thanks for visiting me in my dream. It really meant a lot to me and I cherish that visit.

Don't feel bad for missing things. It is okay if you don't walk me down the aisle on my wedding day or that you're at my high school graduation or even my 8th grade graduation. You're there in spirit, and those will be the best days ever.

Just remember one thing... that you will always be my hero, and that I love you with all my heart.

Love,
Your Little Princess,
a.k.a. Daddy's Girl =
Veronica + Dad.

Veronica,

I'm so glad that you were able to share your story with me, and it is my hope that you found this process to be therapeutic at the same time.

When I think of you, in addition to thinking how extremely creative and entertaining you are on stage, I want to make sure that you do not hold yourself responsible for your father's death. It was by no means your fault, in any way, shape, or form. I am sorry you had to be there to witness him sick.

Please don't blame yourself. I know in talking with you through this process, that you shoulder a lot of guilt surrounding his passing. It is my intent to help you understand that he was sick before your mother went to the store. He had a medical issue going on inside him before she left...something that could not have resulted in any other way. So, please stop blaming yourself and instead focus on the times that you shared with him. Focus on the love that he has for you. Focus on how much he loves you from beyond and how much he is with you everyday.

Change your focus to that which is true. What I just stated is true...and worrying that if you had called 911 earlier that it would have changed the outcome is irrelevant. It wouldn't have changed the outcome. It was his fate, and it was your fate to experience this loss. It must be noted that this is my fate to share with you that his loss is only temporary and to make you realize that he is with you and that you will undoubtedly meet again. Remember the words of Mother Teresa, my dear. "Yesterday is gone. Tomorrow has not yet come. We have only today. Let us begin."

Don't live in the past, honey...change your thoughts and make each day a happy one.

By the way, your participation in this book is your tribute to him. You don't have to worry about that. Well done, my dear. Best of luck to you always!

Much love, Ms. Romero :)

# 5

# PLAY HARD...DIE YOUNG

I'M SAWYER AND I just turned fifteen years old. I was born and raised in Castro Valley, California. For fun I enjoy playing video games. I actually come from a family of gamers. My favorite series is the *Legend of Zelda*, but it'll probably change by the time you read this.

I don't like school very much, but I will do what I have to. It hasn't always been that way. I used to refuse to go to school. In elementary school, I would get picked on, and I was an outcast. I hung out with other outcasts and my neighbors across the way. People didn't seem to like to hang around us much. It was tough growing up, but it's easier to block out the mean things they said. I actually repress all of the negative things from back then, so I couldn't tell you what they said.

I currently live with my loving foster care mother in Modesto, California. This is because my father was murdered on June 26, 2008. I was only 10, and I had just finished 5th grade.

My dad Chris was 32 when he was taken from us. He was a strong, proud person. He always protected the people he cared about, and he made sure that whomever he was around was safe.

The people who worked around my dad called him the "Junkyard Dog" because they felt safe around him. He always liked wearing his hair in a ponytail, and you could always find him in sweats, a long t-shirt, and/or a jacket.

It started off as a good day; I was watching *National Treasure 2* with my step-mom, her sister, and their father. Everything was great until my stepmom started pacing back and forth with a worried look on her face. I brushed it off my shoulders; I didn't put much thought into it or didn't think about it. I decided then to go next door to walk the neighbor's dogs because I got paid to do it. I returned from the dogs and went back into my apartment. As I played Game Cube with my friend for a little bit, my step-mom's dad, Don, was slicing up some pineapple in the kitchen, and he served me mine with sugar. My favorite.

When I stepped back outside, I noticed my grandpa sitting in a black jeep. I wondered, "What is he doing here?" When I walked up to the car, my grandfather was looking at me with a distraught look on his face.

"I have some bad news," he said. As he uttered those words, I stood in shock. "Your father has been shot; he's brain dead."

Once I heard those words, the world closed down on me, and I started to black out. I was ten-years-old at the time. It felt like something was missing, like there was a hole in my body, and I remained sad for months afterwards. The loss was too much to handle. It was loneliness—too sudden. The world collapsed. The realization I would never see him again was paralyzing. I wasn't able to cry about it; I was in denial. I shut down. We had plans. I remembered he was supposed to take me to Val's, a famous restaurant in Castro Valley, for graduating elementary school.

The last time I was with him, we went to Costco. I complained to him, "I don't want to go to Costco. You take too long."

But I still went. Afterwards, he dropped me off at home and left to work. I told him, "I love you, and have fun at work." He was shot and killed later on that day.

Since his murder date, I immediately began living with my uncle; he took me in until I was put in foster care. Why wasn't I allowed to go live with my biological mother, you wonder? It's complicated.

Life, in general, wasn't easy for me before he passed away. My dad would take me to punish my mom. I was a prisoner in his game. He hurt me to hurt her. He loved me though. But he liked to use me to hurt her. He would hurt me to torment and make my mom feel bad. He once told me that my mom didn't love me anymore, that she had another family, and that she didn't want to see me anymore. When he did those things, my mom would break down and cry. The struggle between the two started even before I was born, and it didn't end until he died.

My mom and I lived in fear of what he would do. My little brother is still with my mom to this day. He's only 8, and his name is Ezrah. I'm not with them because my dad told lies about my mom in court. They put her in jail on Mother's Day. My mom is currently working with court to get me back under her roof. I am really looking forward to this. My brother can be annoying, but I still love him.

Why wasn't I with her right away, you may still wonder? Dad was always putting roadblocks up, constantly to keep my mom away from me. She stopped fighting for me because of it. But now that's he's gone, she's fighting her hardest to get me back.

I've been in foster care for three and a half years in Patterson and 4 or 5 months in Modesto. My most recent foster mom has really been there for me. I love her. When I first came to her, the life was sucked out of me. But now I have hope. I show up to school. My grades have gotten better. I'm happier. I have hope that I will one day be back with my mom.

My dad sold Hydroponics. Hydroponics are used to grow weed, and he was killed over his customer layout sheet of where his customers lived and what equipment they bought.

During the altercation that caused my dad's death, the murderers wanted my dad's client list, so they could ultimately steal the weed. They argued because my dad would NOT give them the papers, and they threatened to kill him. My dad said with a gun pointed at him, "Do what you got to do."

He was shot. A homeless person witnessed it. This homeless person knew my dad, and my dad would sometimes feed this guy pizzas (the homeless guy pretty much lived there). The homeless guy saw the murderers with a person I suspect they worked for. Again, this person wanted the clientele info so he could steal weed. A week later, the people on the list were robbed. My mom said she was watching the news one day, and it popped up.

As for the funeral, it started out with the minister asking everyone to rise for a moment of silence, and when I looked around, I found out that I had a lot of family members. It's funny that death would be the only thing that brought us together. It was the first time I've ever seen them, and I've never seen them again.

When the minister asked if anyone would like to say a few words, I got up. I don't remember what I said, but I do remember almost sobbing while I was up there, and I started crying when I sat back down. After a couple of other people talked, the funeral was over. I can't remember much of the funeral. Just that there were old pictures of him put up, no current pictures, and there were flowers for him. My father was cremated.

Once I got outside, I found out that people wouldn't let my mom inside for his service, and they forced her out. My uncle told me afterwards that my mom showed up, but they wouldn't let her in. I don't know why though. It was probably about what my dad said in court. He lied and said that she was a drug addict.

Long after his passing almost a couple years later, I was able to talk to my mom. We talked about my dad and what happened. She said she loved him; she didn't want him to die like that; and she felt it was coming because of his lifestyle.

As for me, it's easier to shut down. I know I can still tell my dad I love him, but I'd rather just not think about it.

If I had been able to go to my mom right afterwards, I would have been more prepared to handle such a loss. If I could change anything, I would make it so my dad wouldn't have sold hydroponics. He worked with hydroponics, and I wish he hadn't because … well, you know. If I could give advice to anyone suffering a loss, I would tell them to try and think of their loved ones when they were happy.

Dad, if you can read this from where you're at, here goes:

Dear Dad,

Even though sometimes I didn't like being around you, either disappointed in you or angry with you, I still love you, and I wish things could've happened in a different way.

I know you tried to get the best out of me, and I wish I could've said goodbye before they cremated you.

Just know that I will always miss you, Dad.

I love you.

Love,

Bubba a.k.a. Soy

Sweet Sawyer,

First of all, I'm so sorry for your loss. I must say I feel so blessed to have been able to meet you. I know that I didn't have the opportunity to teach you per se, but I believe our paths crossed for a reason. I knew from the moment I saw you that you had a sad story, and I thank you for having the courage to share it with me, and ultimately the masses. By doing so, it will undoubtedly provide peace to other young kids who may be going through what you experienced.

When I think about you, Sawyer, the word "decisions" comes to my mind. Decisions.

Your life has been greatly impacted by decisions that your parents have made. What's important to remember is those decisions that impacted your life the most... weren't the best decisions. The judgment that they used doesn't diminish the love that I'm sure they had for you at all. I am certain that they adored you. I mean, who couldn't? You're absolutely adorable. It's just that in life, sometimes people make lousy decisions.

How can we turn your story around? You can learn that each decision, no matter how big or small, creates an action and understand that each action has a consequence. This is important.

"It is not the magnitude of our actions, but the amount of love that is put into them that matters." ~Mother Teresa

If you make decisions based on love, you can't go wrong, Sawyer. You'll start to look at potential outcomes and choose what's best for you. Show your daddy, who is undoubtedly behind our meeting that you are growing up into a great human being. Show him how to get it done right. He is watching; trust me. He is only a thought away. He was taken from you much too soon, but you will certainly meet him again.

Thank you for sharing your story, Sawyer. I'm so blessed to know you and look forward to seeing your future decisions unfold into greatness.

Much love, Ms. Romero

# 6

# HE WAS MORE OF A FATHER

MY NAME IS Rebecca, but I like to be called Becca. I was born in Campbell, California, but now live in Modesto, California. My interests are drawing, blogging, listening to music, hanging out with my close friends, and going to concerts. My hobbies are writing songs, poetry, stories, and sometimes quotes. I also enjoy playing guitar even though I'm not the greatest at it. My view of school is that I'm not too fond of going much, but I try to make the best out of it as possible. My personality is a bit on the shy and awkward side. Most the time I tend to be quiet, while with friends sometimes, I'm outgoing and loud. My taste in music is different from a lot of people, and I listen to anything that is not on the radio.

It was well known that my grandfather was ill, and I was probably 12 or 13 when I found out. My great grandfather was like my father and was more of a father to me than my real dad ever was. My grandpa died from kidney failure in June of 2010.

My grandfather served in World War II and was captured by one of the invading armies but was later rescued. He was American and 81-years-old when he passed away. Willard was his name, but we called him Will for short.

He was a wonderful and much needed father figure in my life. He always supported me on the wackiest things. He would sometimes spoil me since I was the youngest of my mom's three kids. He was, in general, a great man, and his spirit shall live on through the family.

As far as talking about his death before he passed away, not much was said. It was pretty much unspoken of, but what my grandmother did tell me was that granddaddy told her that he was sleeping one night and he met God in Heaven. That was few days before he actually passed away. I tried to stay calm about it. I tried to hide my emotions and not act weak. However, in reality, I wanted to cry, pray, and stuff like that.

When he passed away, it was almost right in front of me. I felt weak. I still regret to this day for not taking the time out of that short time frame to talk to him more and tell him how much he means to me. When he passed, I didn't cry until maybe a few days later. Every now and again when I remember, it makes me want to cry, not always though, just most of the time. I miss him and think of him a lot when I hear the name Will or Grandpa or something. He was my father and grandfather, and I miss his happiness and positive mood in bad situations.

We didn't have the money at the time for a funeral, so there wasn't one. He also wanted his body donated to science, so we had them make the leftover parts into ashes, which my grandmother still has today.

Since his passing, I experienced a dream once where I was at the scene where he sadly passed away. He appeared in front of me as his younger sort of self. He looked so much healthier than he did before he passed. In my dream, he looked stronger; he was no longer shaking with his hands, and he had some hair. He said not to worry about what I had been regretting since he passed, about me not telling him how much he meant to me. He said he already knew it without me saying a word. Then, he vanished.

I felt a little sad, yet relieved and a little bit of mixed emotions. Was that for real or fake? It seemed real to me, but all I know is that it could be my mind playing tricks on me. But then there have been other signs.

Once there was this song that I found while streaming through Pandora radio on one of my stations. I heard a song from the band JamesTown Story. It came on, and it instantly reminded me of my grandfather. Like it was a message from him to me:

"I can't wait to see the day,
when the tears all go away...."

as well as a message from me back to him if that makes any sense.

"I did nothing at all, it's all my fault you're gone,
Your face on my wall,
it tells it all,
you will live on..."

Another example of feeling him close is that I live with my grandmother. She has his ashes in a box in her room. So, his remains are at the house right? Sometimes in the middle of the night, I feel that there is someone behind me, or watching over me. Sometimes it saddens me because he was never buried, but yet it does comfort me knowing he is close by me at all times.

We honor him since his passing. On the first year without him on Thanksgiving, we set out a plate on the table where he would usually sit before he became ill, bedridden, and passed away. Yes, it did bring comfort somewhat knowing we still remembered him and that we reminisced about him. How we miss him and that he's in a better place now was expressed and this honoring him brought me comfort.

What would have helped me prepare for his loss would have been to talk to him more and to better understand death in general. Death is the unknown. If I could change anything, I would have been there more for him his last few days. Then I could have gotten everything off my chest and told him everything that he meant to me.

If I could give any advice to someone suffering a loss or about to suffer a loss, I would say that it might seem hard to handle it at first, but it will get better over time. It really depends on how you are taking the loss. But it does get easier, I promise.

---

*Dear Grandpa Will,*

*I miss you and hope you're having a wonderful time up in Heaven, if there is one, ya know? I love you dearly, and I am sorry for not spending much time with you your last few days. Words cannot express how much I miss you. It's been about 3 to 4 years since you've been gone. I'm gonna keep this short. I love you so much, and have a wonderful time now, you hear?*

*Love, Becca*

---

Dearest Becca,

What a year! I am so glad that you were in my advisory and English classes this year! You are truly a sweetheart, and I truly enjoyed getting to know you. I'm so glad that you agreed to be a part of this book project. I know that it was your grandfather who passed, but in this day and age, families aren't the same as they used to be. Sometimes grandparents become the parent especially when the biological parent is not doing what he or she should be doing. Thank goodness for Willard.

I especially loved your segment, and I love the fact that grandpa came to you in a dream. What a gift! I especially love how open you are to receiving signs from spirit. It is when we are open to receiving signs that the most messages come through. I find messages from spirit are the most fulfilling and bring me great peace. I know there is nothing to fear in the afterlife as I too have received multiple messages from spirit.

Continue to honor Grandpa; he is there in spirit. Continue to believe… because you will meet again. It is having this knowledge that makes death not as terrifying as a participant, and it is also reassuring that our loved ones are only a thought away. Remember…

"No one ever really dies as long as they took the time to leave us with fond memories." ~ Chris Sorensen

Grandpa did that, and for that you are blessed.

Best of luck to you, sweet Becca.

Much love, Ms. Romero

# 7

## Two Moms Gone

I'M JUSTYN, A fifteen-year-old born in Los Gatos, California, who moved to Modesto in the first grade. I have an older sister who is three years older than I am, and I love to bowl. I want to be a professional bowler when I grow up. I have been playing since I was eleven. As a competitive level bowler, I have been told that I may get a bowling scholarship. I also play video games during my free time when I'm not bowling. Sometimes I play so much that I get lightheaded, and the only thing I read are the video game manuals, so I know how to play and win the game. My dream girl is Ariana Grande—she is so hot! One day...

Anyway, my mom's name was Jennifer, and she was 27 when she passed away from leukemia. She battled for a short few months. I was two-years-old when my mom was taken away from me by the evil c-word.

I thought my grandma was my mom because I didn't realize what happened to my actual mom. I was just too young. My grandmother, who I thought was my mother, got sick a year later after my mom. We all lived together my entire life. My mom, sister, and I lived with my grandfather and grandmother. When my grandmother Linda died, I would always write letters to her about how much I loved her. I was about three or four when that happened—two moms gone in a two-year period.

My grandfather, mom's dad, adopted me after she passed away. Now Grandpa Ron was raising my sister and me. Grandpa was working two jobs to take care of us. He did a lot of thinking; he went to church a lot. He had a renewed an interest in church due to what was happening in his life. I was obviously too young to know what was going on at the time. But since then, I was about five when my grandpa explained it to me. He just told me. I was sad, and I cried. I believe I understood what death was and what he was talking about. He has always said, "She is in a better place."

He still misses them both to this day. I mean… he lost his wife and daughter. I have never really spoken to my grandfather about it since the first time when I was five. It was too difficult, and it made me sad, so I didn't talk about it. My sister, when she was nine, would talk about it with me like everyday about how much she missed her. She missed being held and explained to me how my mom was because I never really knew her. My sister showed me the letters.

I have letters from my mother to my sister and me that she wrote before she passed away. The letters stated how much she loved us and that she wished that she wasn't sick and that she could stay longer to take care of us. The letters are in her handwriting, and I will cherish those letters forever. I'm connected to her when I read them.

I was too young to remember either of the funerals, but my grandpa takes us to San Jose to the cemetery where they are buried right next to each other whenever he has the time. For her birthday, we go out to eat at my mother's favorite place The Macaroni Grill in San Jose.

As for my dreams, I've seen her in one when I was in the fourth grade. In the dream, I wake up and go to watch TV. My mom suddenly walks in and sits on the couch. She started saying how she loves me and how grandpa is going to take care of me, and that everything is going to be all right. I woke up crying, and I told my grandpa about it. He says, "It's alright. She loves you very much." After the crying, I was happy about her visit.

My aunt dreams about my grandma and has seen her too. Not too long ago, she physically saw her in her house. My aunt and her baby were in their house lying down on the bed and heard the door open. She started speaking to her mom and said, "Mom, if that's you, flicker the lights or something, and she did." The next day she actually saw her. She started crying and panicked and called Grandpa and told him what happened. Grandpa was really happy about it, and he went to her house to talk about it.

I think about her a lot. A couple of months ago, I went to Calvary to watch "Heaven's Gate, Hell's Flames" and I cried through the whole thing. It made me think of my mom. I missed her. I thought about her and her journey after death. It was all so confusing. A week later, I went there again to Calvary and prayed for my mom. I sat there with my head down the entire time, and all the workers prayed for me too.

Both my sister and I have a picture of my mom in our room. We also have a book of all the things we've done together. For example, like pictures, souvenirs, and stuff from our trip to Disneyland.

Looking back, knowing how everything turned out, I would have told my mom and grandma that I loved them more. As for my mom, I wish I knew what she was going through so I would have cherished every moment of our time together. I was just too young.

If someone is going through it, it is tough. I would recommend that if you have a parent who is very sick and going to pass, suggest to your parent to write you letters so they can always be close to you. So you have a piece of them. I sincerely wish you the best. I will pray for you. But please make sure you tell him or her everything you need to, and don't worry, dude, my mom came back to me and it will happen. Just be open to it.

———

Dear Mom,

I think about you a lot, and I wonder if you're up in Heaven with Grandma.

Please come and visit me more in my dreams. I really enjoyed the first visit and long for more chances to reunite with you. I consider you my guardian angel and know that you're with me.

Please help me achieve my goals. I hope to make you proud. I will try my best to be the best for you.

Love you forever, your baby, Justyn

———

Dear Nana,

I miss you so much. I loved watching movies with you at night. Sorry for taking so long to fall asleep and having to make you watch movies as a result. I just loved sleeping with you guys.

Also, thank you for taking care of my mother when she was sick. I'm sure it was a hard thing to do, watching your baby pass away. You spent 24/7 in the hospital with her and thank you for all the love that you gave her.

Nana, please watch over my grandpa and make sure he doesn't get sick. To lose him would be the worst thing ever. I don't know where I'd go.

Nana, you were a mom to me, and I will be forever your son. I love you and continue to watch over from above. Please.

Love, Justyn

My dearest Justyn,

I'm so blessed to have had the opportunity to be a part of your life. I believe that you were sent to me, and please know that I am always here for you. You've been dealt a tough hand in life, and I am sincerely amazed at how you were able to keep it together. Must be your two guardian angels up above! I am certain of it!

My words of wisdom for you would be... Please... don't follow in the footsteps of your father and learn from the mistakes of those before you. As life gets tough, demand more of yourself and do life right the first time.

Think about that please. This may be your one lesson to learn in this lifetime—how to overcome such obstacles. It is my firm belief that if we don't learn our life lesson during this lifetime, we must return to experience it all over again until we get it right. Now, does that sound like fun to you?

I didn't think so.

You have a heart of gold and please allow others to get close to you. It took a while for me to crack you, and I'm so glad that you shared your love for your mom and grandma with me. I hope I was able to help you, and whenever you look at the picture frame I gave you of your mother and you, I hope it reminds you of your middle school teacher who thinks that you are amazing.

Keep in touch, Justyn. I look forward to seeing you grow up into adulthood, to finding a career, and to living an amazing life.

Much love,
Ms. Romero :)

# 8

# FRIENDS FOREVER

I'M HOLLY, A fourteen-year-old who lost my best friend Victoria.

I had sent her a birthday card, and when I signed, I put "Love, your sis." We were so close, practically sisters. When she was in the car accident that killed her, she had the letter in the car with her. The police officer told me, "… It looked like she just opened it."

When the accident occurred, they sent everyone to the hospital, and they searched the car to find someone to contact right away. They found her phone with her dad's number in it, and they also found my letter to her and the envelope. Since I signed "your sis" they assumed I was her older sister and with my address on the envelope they knew where to find me. They sent an officer to my house to inform me right away. When they told me, I felt as if I had been there with her. I was ten-years-old when she died.

To learn of this loss was the most devastating thing in the world. The feelings of insecurity and disbelief were dispersed throughout my entire body. Every limb in my body begged to give up and let me collapse onto the floor. It felt as if my heart was stuck in my throat just pounding and pounding and pounding, waiting to burst out and flop on the floor, only to sink in my endless ocean of tears. The ocean of horror and uncertainty that stunned me continued to drown me for months to come.

The funeral was small and short, but altogether sweet. Although I would have loved to participate in the funeral, I was not asked. During the funeral I was still really upset and unsure about my real feelings. There were times of sadness, but then there were times of comfort where I felt secure for once, and I knew she was in a better place. Altogether in the end, I left with a sense of comfort, but I still became upset whenever her death was mentioned.

The funeral was held in a small chapel where she had her Baptism. The chapels had a lot of windows, but it was dark inside because it had rained, and there was no sunshine. There were candles lit to provide more light. The walls of the chapel were dark beige, and the chapel had a high ceiling. We sat in pews during the service, and the stage was adorned with a bunch of flowers and pictures of her and her family.

I remember almost the entire funeral, but the clearest memory was when her dad was speaking and said, "Let these tears not be tears of sadness but tears of joy, for they're now in Heaven enjoying all God has insured them."

Three months after the funeral, Victoria returned to me in one of my dreams. In my dream, it was windy, I was in my backyard on the swings, and she appeared next to me. She told me that she missed me, and that she would be looking forward to helping me. Then she told me to tell her dad to check the bottom of the dresser, under the socks. I didn't get what she meant. She delivered the message that she would help me, and that her dad needed to look at the bottom of her dresser under the socks. When I woke up I was overjoyed but scared because I didn't know if it was real or not.

I told her dad, and when he checked he found his wife's wedding ring and his daughter's pictures. These items were missing, and he had been looking for them for months. Can you imagine that? She came to me with this message for her father. I'm still blown away.

Victoria and I were in musicals together when we were younger, and every year we did an annual show based on the 50s. One year in the show we did the song "Rockin' Robin." That was her favorite number and soon after favorite song. One day I was at the store, and I heard this song playing. I was like this is weird, it's 2011 and they're playing a song from the 50s. Then later that evening at a Downey football game, I heard the song again for one of their homecoming floats. Their costumes also looked like the ones we used in our annual musical. I was freaking out because I kept hearing it day after day. It just didn't make sense. Then one day I saw an advertisement for tickets to the annual musicals I used to perform in. The song came on again, I knew it meant something, so I asked my mom if I could get a ticket, and she said okay.

So, on the night of the performance I went and watched the musical. Their final number was "Rockin' Robin." I could not figure out why this song was playing. While I was trying to figure it out the director started talking, and at the end of her speech, she did the dedications as always. "This year the performance is only dedicated to one person..." she said. Then she announced, "... Victoria Johnson."

I was shocked! They performed in memory of her. After she explained why, half of the crowd was in tears, and we moved into the lobby.

I met with the director afterwards, and she remembered me. We were talking for a while when she said that she had something for me. She reached into her pocket and pulled out a hair ribbon.

At first, I was confused, but then I looked closer and it had Victoria Johnson stitched into it. It was the ribbon she had used when she participated in the musicals. We all had one with our name on it, but why did she have hers? She looked at me and said, "Remember when I said you couldn't keep them because I said I had to reuse them? Well, I used them tonight, but not hers. I saved it in her honor. Just for you."

She looked at me and said she wanted me to have it. When I took it, I asked her how she knew I was going to be here. She said she didn't. She just had a feeling. Then she walked away.

I felt a connection to Victoria. I finally saw that she was always going to be with me. I spent so much time thinking that my life was terrible that I didn't bother to see that she wanted me to push through the pain and continue my life like she was still there. To live the life that she wanted me to live. The life we always talked about as little kids with adventure, happiness, friends, secrets, and dreams that were too big to accomplish.

One day, my family got a new car, and then my parents took us, my brothers and me, all out to ice cream. When we were done we went back to the car, and when I opened the door, a locket fell out. It was a locket Victoria had given me. How did it get into our NEW car? I opened it, and our picture was on one side, and on the other side was an inscription. It read, "Always love, always hold on, always remember, me!" To this very day, I still don't know how it got there, but every time I hold it, I remember all of our moments together.

Every year on her birthday, I go and eat at her favorite restaurant and ice cream shop. (That is where we always went together.) After that, I go and visit her father.

What would have helped me mentally prepare for this loss is being able to spend more time with her, knowing of the loss before it happened, and/or getting a proper goodbye.

I would have talked about my loss more, not have been so rude to people, and comforted others rather than ignoring them. They were only trying to comfort me. I shouldn't have been so rude.

My advice to others in a similar situation would be to not hold on to your feelings. It only makes it worse, it's okay to cry, and this wasn't your last goodbye. You'll see them again someday.

Since I know you are watching over me, this is for you:

*Dear Victoria,*

*You are the best friend a person could ever have. It was a joy seeing you change from that shy little girl in the corner to the inspiring, outgoing young woman you became. I miss you so much! Life is hard without you, but I feel better knowing that you're watching over me.*

*Thanks for the messages in dreams and through music. Keep them coming. I also miss your compassion and your unforgettable laugh. I treasure every moment I had with you, and there will always be room for you in my heart.*

*You're the sister I never had. My only regret to you is not getting to say happy birthday to you for the last time.*

*Thanks for all the years of our friendship.*

*Much love,*
*Holly (Sis)*

*Good Golly Miss Holly!*

*Young lady, I think you are one sensitive young lady. Not sensitive in the sense that your feelings get hurt easily, but sensitive in the sense that you are open to what lies beyond our realm and to receiving messages from spirit. Both stories exhibit significant visits from those who have crossed over. Your maturity in how you view and explain them is unlike most your age. You get it. You are wise beyond your years.... I love it!*

*I already know how brilliant you are academically as well as how talented and creative you are! I'm not one iota worried about you and how you are going to turn out. You have your head on straight and can pretty much attain whatever your heart desires. That's how well-rounded, focused, and dedicated you are!*

*That being said: don't go changing. From a favorite book of mine The Outsiders, Holly, "Stay gold." You're gold, girl.*

*Thank you for sharing your story.*

*Much love,*

*Ms. Romero :)*

# 9

---

# TAKEN IN FRONT OF ME

I'M BRIANA, A fourteen-year-old going into the ninth grade. I'm Portuguese, tall with braces on my teeth and olive skin. I am an only child who was born and raised in Modesto, California. I lived in Hilmar for two and a half years, but I have predominantly lived in Modesto.

I love to hang out with my friends going to the movies, bowling, hanging out at the park, and playing sports: soccer, softball, and volleyball. I listen to a lot of music: "22" by Taylor Swift, "Roman Revenge" by Nikki Minaj and Eminem, and Mario's "Let Me Love You." I have the hugest crush on Taylor Lautner. I'm your typical average teenage girl. I love to laugh and have fun, and my mother was murdered on September 27, 2001.

What I know about my mom, I've learned from my family members. I know that she loved the color purple and that her favorite flower was the lily. I know she had a collection of china dolls because my room was filled with them. Unlike me, she was not into sports. Her name was Lillian, and she was thirty-one when she was murdered. A friend shot her and then shot himself.

Unfortunately, I was present at the time of her murder and this I remember vividly. I was in the living room, which was adjacent to the kitchen where it occurred. I was watching the show *PB&J* on the Playhouse Disney channel.

They were talking in the kitchen, and it kept getting louder and louder. My mother was standing in the doorway of the kitchen and the living room where I was, and I could see her. She looked irritated. They were having a discussion and then I heard the first gunshot. It hit her in the butt area. She was getting away from him. The gunshot was at butt level so had she not been standing there, I would have been hit. The second gunshot was also from behind and hit her in the back going straight into her heart. I saw the second one hit her, and I watched her fall to the ground.

I never saw him, the person my mom was arguing with. Next thing I heard was another gunshot and a big old thunk. I learned later that he had shot himself. That thud must have been him hitting the ground.

I had a feeling that she was gone. I was crying. Neighbors heard the gunshot and me crying and called the police. It seemed like I was alone for a while. It was a couple minutes into the show when the gunshots went off and when the police arrived that show was finished. I was almost finished with my second episode. During that entire time, I was crying. I walked up to her and tried to wake her up. I pushed on her. She didn't respond. I just sat there, next to her, close by.

The police arrived and took me to the station until late. With the police officers, I calmed down a little. I felt better.

On the other side of town, my dad, grandma, and everyone was looking for my mom and me. They hadn't heard from us. My dad had heard that there was a shooting in the back of Hilmar High School, but he didn't think it was related to us. Ultimately, my dad found me at ten o'clock at night, and her murder had occurred at 1:30 in the afternoon.

My mom was buried in Turlock near family members. After she passed away, I moved to Modesto to live with my dad and my grandma.

I was almost three when it happened, and I didn't talk for years after the incident. I had speech therapy until second grade to help me speak because I simply shut down and had no verbal ability. I did not formulate sentences, and I couldn't articulate very well. I didn't speak to anyone. NO ONE. I only made Teletubbie noises that I know of.

I know I was sent to counseling for three or four years after the incident, and I remember a sand pit and dinosaurs. I finally started speaking again.

As for school, the first day of third grade I was so shy that I didn't want my dad to leave. It was a new school as well. But things got better for me.

Mother's Days are tough. It's Grandma and Aunt Day for me. I thank them. I visit her gravesite every Mother's Day and sometimes on her birthday. I miss her so much. There is a part of me that doesn't know what she was like. It feels like a part of me is missing.

It is still hard for me sometimes. On Mother's Day, I cry. I think, why can't I be normal? Why can't I have a happy life with both of my parents? I feel like I'm left out because I hear friends say, "Me and my mom are getting our nails done." Then, there is me, the tomboy: watching sports and playing video games, without a mom.

When I was younger, I had recurring nightmares of what happened that day. Then I would have dreams about her in general. I was happy in those dreams; she was with me again and we were reunited. One dream: my mom, aunt, cousin Brooke, and I went to this place, and we were riding ponies. It was a great dream. These dreams came to me in fourth grade. I would wake up thinking it was real, and then I l remembered that it wasn't. No more dreams occurred after fifth grade.

One time when I was nine, I was in my bedroom crying holding a picture of my mom. I was saying, "I wish you were here with me to get me through this."

Just then I felt a weird wind come and touch my leg. Something gently touched my leg from the top to my knee. It kind of freaked me out. I believe it was her. I was inside my room with no windows open. It's cool to think that she can be there.

I appreciate my life more now. If my mom would have moved from where she was standing, I would have been hit by the first bullet.

I really appreciate my dad for always being there for me since my mom's death. He is wonderful, supportive, character building, and loving. He is my rock. He has a soft side; he cried at my mom's grave a while ago. I look up to him and adore him so much. Thanks, Dad, for everything. Thanks for putting up with me for all these years.

If you are reading this and you have lost your parent or are about to lose your parent, I would tell you to spend as much time as you can with your parents cause you don't know what is going to happen next. Enjoy the moments, and make memories with each other before they pass.

If they are already gone, keep your head up, because they are in Heaven watching you and leading you to a better life. Your emotions will change with different occasions, such as laughing at a funny story or sadness after a lonely Mother's Day, but know that you're not alone. There are other people just like you and me who have lost their mom or dad at a young age. When you're sad, talk it out with other family members and ask them questions about what they were like. Watch home movies and look at old photos. It makes them seem real and that they were here for you. Helps you recall old memories, and also consider this: there will always be new people coming into your life.

---

Dear Mom,

Thanks, Mom, for giving me life and letting me be where I am today. I know since your crossing, I had a real hard time getting over it. Don't feel bad that I had to see you die like that. It built a lot of character, and it made me who I am now, and the woman I am becoming.

I think about you non-stop, and my love for you will never end! I am so grateful for a mom like you because you were always kind, generous, tall, beautiful, and from what I hear, a great dancer.

I hope you are proud of all my accomplishments in school, sports, chores, and in life. I believe that we will meet again in the afterlife and be a happy family. Boy, that will be a great day.

Please watch over my dad for me. I need him in my life.

I love you, Mom.

Love, Briana

---

Little Miss Briana,

My goodness, what a brave young woman you are! My heart breaks for little Briana and what you had to experience. Thank you for sharing your story with the world, and I'm sure there are many others who have witnessed such an atrocity who feel like they are the only one who had to go through something horrible like this.

*That being said: trust that your mother is with you always. Whether you like it or not, she is with you. She is a thought away, and I'm certain that she is so proud of how you have lived your life thus far. You are the sweetest girl with a smile that lights up a room, so kind and such a generous soul. A true delight to be around!*

*Your father is a great man and a personal friend of mine. The love that he feels for you is evident to anyone that is in his life. YOU are his love and you are so lucky to have your daddy.*

*You are going to do great things, girlfriend. You have rebounded from this experience and no one would even suspect that you suffered through such a tragedy. I attribute that to your internal strength and a very loving family. You are truly blessed, Briana. Others aren't as lucky to have an extended family like yours.*

*I can't wait to see you blossom into a beautiful woman and learn of what you become. I know it will be something amazing. Your track record shows that you are right on track.*

*Much love to you, girl. Thanks for sharing your very private story, and may the force be with you always.*

*Ms. Romero :)*

# 10

## MY LOYAL CARETAKER AND BEST FRIEND

I'M RILEY, A thirteen-year-old going into ninth grade next year. I always strive to be a good person and to help people, which is why I'm sharing my story.

I really enjoy drawing, and I have been drawing since birth. It is sincerely my happiest memory; one could always find me in a corner drawing by myself, even today. For fun, I also collect Manga, coins, and poker chips. My favorite movies are the Ace Ventura series because I simply love animals, and I feel that I can communicate with them.

As for siblings, I have a younger sister who is three years younger and a half brother seven years older than myself whom I adore.

Currently, I'm doing the best I've ever done in school. This last report card I earned three A's, one B, and two C's. My favorite subjects are History and Art, of course.

As a child, I was very depressed. I would always stay alone in my room and play with Polly Pockets to pretend I was happy.

I wasn't really happy though because my dad would hurt my feelings. I'm sure that he didn't intend to do that, but as a young child that is how it came across.

I must tell you that my life changed dramatically when I was four. I lost my grandfather who was my best friend and a man that I loved dearly.

Grampy was special for several reasons. He was always generous and considerate. As a young man and into adulthood, he worked in construction and would rarely, if ever, leave work; he was so responsible. He did leave once, however, to come and help my mother turn on the headlights of her new car. It's actually kind of funny. She would tell me about this, since it happened before I was born. She was "spazzed" out, calling Grampy and asking him how to turn on the headlights in her car. He, in turn, left his job to rescue her, and he never left work! That's the kind of man he was.

Although Grampy could never really afford to take us places, once a month he would take us out to McDonalds. My mom had me eating extremely healthy, so that would be his little treat for Wes and me.

If he came to the house, sometimes he would bring milkshakes for us. So drinking a milkshake always reminds me of the good memories I shared with him.

I always sat on Grampy's lap. He sat on his big recliner with both Wes and me on his lap. We watched movies and Boomerang. Boomerang was the TV channel that aired the shows my mom would watch when she was young. We would also do puzzles together as a family on Grampy's dining table. Our time together was simply wonderful.

A special memory I have is that he served glasses of chocolate milk for Wes and me, and we would use a licorice stick as a straw. He would drink it the same way! I even remember the huge tub of licorice on his end table. He also had a big cuckoo clock, and it would crack me up when I was little. As annoying as the cuckoo sound was, Grampy would constantly set it to midnight, so he could hear my laughter.

I spent most of my time with him. Grampy always took care of my older brother and me. (My grandmother died before I was born, so all I knew was my Grampy.) My mother and father were always working hard to support us and didn't have enough time to take care of us, so, of course, Grampy stepped in to help. No matter what happened, he was always there. Grampy was the one to drop everything for us.

I was four-years-old when my Grampy Larry passed away, and my brother was eleven. The night it happened my brother called Grampy's home phone, which he always did before going to sleep, and he never picked up. He continued to call him, but there was no answer.

My brother informed my mom, "Something's wrong! He won't pick up. We have to go check up on him!"

My mother told him not to worry, that he was fine and that he was just sleeping. She had never been so wrong. Several days passed, and my uncle went to go check up on him.

Grampy was found lying on his kitchen floor, dead with his glass of water near the refrigerator. He died of a heart attack.

Now, mind you. I was never told that he died. Mom was nervous, panicking, and my bro knew something was up. My mother told us Grampy had moved, and we couldn't see him anymore. I felt she was lying, and so did my brother. My brother knew I couldn't handle this type of news, so he held me tight and told me everything would be all right.

Grampy died in 2004 and there wasn't a funeral that I know of. My uncle had him cremated. He still has his ashes to this day.

If there was a memorial service for him, I didn't go and that makes me sad.

As a result of this confusion, I think I have trust issues. It is difficult to open up my heart to people because I always wonder if someone is lying to me.

Well, weeks later after the death/move, my entire family came to clear out his house. As for me, I felt my life was over, and my best friend was gone. I got even quieter. I didn't watch TV anymore. I would sit in my room and cry to myself. I retreated. I would hold the teddy bear my brother gave me and hope nothing more would happen.

His death was an extreme shock to my brother and me, even though I felt something would eventually happen to him. Grampy was a heavy smoker, and even at my young age, I knew something would happen.

After Grampy was gone for a month or two, I received another devastating blow. My mom came and reluctantly told me that Wesley was going to be leaving us and moving in with his father!

WHAT?

I had never felt so alone! I had now lost my two closest friends! I loved my brother! How could this be happening? I was so hurt.

With Grampy gone, I was now sent to a Catholic childcare place where I knew no one. At night, I returned home to find my mom gone at work and my dad busy with his own projects and his buddies. I, as a result, retreated to my bedroom alone.

In the first grade, I found myself always drawing Grampy, Wes, and myself. We were always happy in the drawings. I wouldn't do my schoolwork; I simply drew that same picture. I had never felt so much pain and sadness before in my entire life. My closest friend was dead, I had been lied to, my brother was gone, and I was a mess throughout my next few years of school. I couldn't focus in class. I was tested for ADHD, ADD, and autism. I always had mental breakdowns and started crying because I couldn't stop drawing my Grampy, Wes, and I together again. Now that I'm older, thank goodness, I have gotten much better.

As for visits, the night before Grampy's death, I had a dream that I was with Grampy and my brother. We were together at his house playing with my brother's Transformers and having fun. There was no dialogue between us—he was completely mute—and it shocked me.

I told him, "Grampy, this is fun! Why aren't you talking? You always talk to Wes and me."

I felt like Grampy was scared or nervous, and at the end of the dream, he gave both of us a big hug as I woke up. Could it be that his soul was also coming to say a goodbye to me in the dream? I never told anyone about it until just a few years ago when my uncle came to visit.

My uncle told me that I was going to be okay and that I had a special gift. I'm sensitive to my dreams, to the messages behind them, and to their timing. For instance, the night before Virginia died (my mother's friend and the closest thing I had to a grandmother) I had a dream recalling the first time I met her. I relived the moment in that dream from when I was nine years old. I felt happy and peaceful in that dream. I believe it was as if her soul was saying goodbye.

In another very special dream, my beloved cat Milkshake came to me in a dream. Milkshake and I had a unique bond, and she was my *everything*. I had Milkshake for six years until she lost her life a few months ago in a terrible accident. Unbeknownst to all of us, she had hopped into the washing machine. Was it really an accident? Unfortunately for me, when I was switching the laundry, I found my very best friend dead inside. That absolute, horrific memory haunts me to this day. It was by far the worst thing that I've ever experienced. It destroyed me.

It's very difficult to share this with you all. So, you can imagine my feelings of relief when she visited me in a dream. Milkshake was kneading on my chest and pawing on my face, and I was petting her. She came back to say hello to me, and I was so happy in that moment. I still miss her to this day. My heart aches when I think of my precious Milkshake, and I think of her often.

In regards to timing, I've started to pay attention and notice that every time there is a loss close to me, it occurs in increments of four years. Except for Milkshake, her death came three years early in relation to the previous loss. Maybe it is because she was a cat and it equals out in cat years.

In closing, for all of you who have lost someone dear to you, just remember... they are still with you, even if you can't see them they are there, and they will be there to protect you from harm. I have always felt Grampy's presence around me, and I look forward to future dreams where I can reunite with all of my loved ones.

---

*Dear Grampy,*

*Although I can't see you, I feel that you're still here with me, Grampy. I want to say thank you for everything you have done for Wes and me. I have always felt alone and had no friends. You made me feel important. Even when I was little, I was completely alone except* for your love. Thank you for that. I truly wouldn't be me if it weren't for you making me stronger, and I want to say thank you in front of the whole world. I love you, Grampy.

I just wish I could see you one last time.

Love your granddaughter,

Ri

---

My Dearest Riley,

I feel so fortunate to have crossed your path and love that I was able to meet someone as kind and loving as you are. As I reread your story and having spoken to you about your losses and your life, I stand back in admiration at the strong, young woman that you've become.

This year in particular…I saw a major transformation in you. In the beginning and the middle of the year, you were at times, fragile. This last month or so, I have seen a new Riley, a confident Riley, one who will make it and accomplish great things.

Please try to trust again. Know that your parents were simply trying to protect you due to your extreme bond to your grandfather. I'm certain keeping it a secret wasn't a malicious act. As you grow into a young adult, try to step into their shoes and see where they were coming from and maybe it won't hurt as badly.

Learn from their mistakes as well. We must always be learning from our mistakes and the mistakes of those around us.

I am so sorry for your multiple losses… Grampy crossing over, your brother leaving, and what happened to dear, precious Milkshake. As you stated in your chapter, your loved ones are still with you and will protect you from harm. I wholeheartedly agree with you, my wise friend. I wholeheartedly agree. In the words of renowned psychic medium John Holland, "Your loved ones are just a thought away."

Thank you for sharing your story, Riley. I hope it brought you some peace and that you continue forward in the next chapter of life with a smile on that pretty face. Remember, attitude is everything and happiness comes from within. I'm here for you always.

Much love to you, dear. Please keep in touch.

Love, Ms. Romero :)

# 11

## IF ONLY HE HADN'T GONE

I'M XAVIER, AN 18-YEAR-OLD who was born and raised in Ceres. My sister Breanna was in Ms. Romero's class this year, and it was through her that she found out about the loss of our father.

I'm a typical teen. I really love sports. My teams are the Raiders and Dolphins in football, the Diamond Backs, Oakland A's, and Los Angeles Dodgers in baseball, and the Lakers and Golden State for basketball.

I also consider myself a pretty cool guy. I listen to Fabulous, Kanye West, Big Sean, Mac Dre, Kendrick Lamar, J Stalin, and some electronica.

Eduardo, my dad, also grew up in Modesto, California, and he was the nicest man ever. My father never hit us or yelled at us. He always taught me to do something—how to catch a ball, how to play chess in kindergarten, etcetera....

For work, he was an electrical engineer in the San Jose area.

Off duty, he loved to fish and watch sports such as soccer, football, and basketball. His team was the Dolphins. He was also a pretty good dancer—hip hop, break dance moves, popping, and different stuff.

One thing is for sure—he loved his family, and his friends were considered family. My dad was outgoing, outspoken, and when he was 32-years-old, he was murdered in Mexico.

I remember saying goodbye to him before he left on a business trip for Mexico. For some reason, I had a feeling that he wasn't coming back. I did NOT want him to go! I cried a lot! I kept holding him, and I wouldn't let him go. Finally, my mom had to grab me. She was holding me back because I didn't want him to go.

My dad, unfortunately, was in the drug business. He had driven to Mexico with friends, and what happened was a drug deal gone bad. Soon after, his body was found dead on the desert floor in Juarez, Chihuahua, Mexico. The family was in shock. My uncle, who was a teenager, flew to Mexico as our family representative to identify him.

How I learned of his death is very clear in my mind today. I remember that day perfectly. It was in April and everything was just off in my little world. Things weren't normal when my mom came home with two family friends and they decided to read me a storybook. I thought it was "off" because... why are *all* of them reading me a book?

The book had a dinosaur in it and the topic was about death. It was definitely out of the ordinary. My mom, however, couldn't go through with it, and after a while she just straight up told me, "Dad passed away."

I kind of understood... we were talking about it with the book. The pieces were coming together, but for some reason, I was kind of in denial. I didn't really get that somebody can be gone from your life for forever, you know? I didn't really get the idea. I may have been too young to grasp it, but as I got older, it started to hit me more.

I should also mention that as a young boy, there was a lot of death around me. As a kid, I saw a lot of family dying. My uncle, grandpa, and then my father all died when I was a young boy. My dad's bro killed himself when his relationship failed, and then my grandpa's death. Before grandpa died, I remember seeing him all bloody as he walked into my parents' room. Then, my dad's murder happened in that order.

The Mexican police conducted an investigation on my father's death, but nothing really became of it right away. Years after the incident, on the news I learned that a suspect had been found.

When he was murdered, I was six-years-old and my sister was just a newborn. As I lived without my dad, sometimes I felt like I was to avenge him and get back at those that took him from me. However, now that I'm older, I do not feel the need to retaliate.

There was a funeral for him, and I sat in the front row. Mom was a crying a lot. People were crying everywhere, my grandmother too. I could see him from where I was sitting. It was an open casket and people went up to see him. It was good to see him again. He looked like himself, but to see him not moving, it was like... dang.

I miss my father. Whenever I am in a bad situation I think, "I wish dad was alive."

Since his death, my family members and I have seen him in dreams. One dream he was there and he said, "Come with me... come with me..." My sister woke up and my mom weirded out.

Another instance of his spirit being around is that our keyboard would start typing by itself when no one was near the device.

I had a dream about him once—a very cool dream. We were playing with a ball. He was teaching me how to catch and throw as a young boy again. It was a purple and orange Nerf ball to be exact. The park was endless, and I was purely happy. This dream happened when I was age eleven. I was so happy. I didn't tell anybody about the dream—it was my secret, until now.

On his birthday every year we bring flowers for him, my uncle, and grandpa to the cemetery. I'll sit and talk to him inside my head. I tell him things such as, "Please guide me, I love you, and thank you for everything you've taught me." I do know that everything happens for a reason, and there is something to be learned by losing him.

If I could help another kid going through the loss of a parent, I would tell them that everything happens for reason. That's my philosophy. I see that I have benefitted in maturity from his loss. When you go through life without a dad, whom do you look up to as a male role model? It was a major turning point for me. It was early, but it happened. So yes, even though this is horrible, there is a bright side to losing him. No matter what the situation, there is always a bright side.

I would change nothing as to how I handled my loss. I was open with my dad, and he knew I loved him. So I would change nothing in that respect.

Again, if a parent's death is happening in your life, then obviously you are a strong enough person to pull through. God wouldn't do it to you, unless you could. Another thing: don't mourn for the person—they don't want to see you like that. If you really want to make them happy, be happy yourself.

L i v e   l i f e... how they would want you to live it.

─≈≈≈─

Dear Xavier,

What a great young man you have become! Like you, I am also a firm believer that everything happens for a reason, and I believe there is a reason why your sister was put in my class this year.

When I had you in class years ago, I had no idea of the loss that you had suffered. I wish that I could have helped you back then. However, timing is everything, and you probably weren't ready for such help. The timing of your sister reconnecting me with you years later was meant to be. You were meant to be a part of this book, and I'm so glad that you are sharing your story with the world.

You suffered a tremendous loss, losing your dad, and you have turned that loss into a positive. BRAVO to you! That shows such strength, insight, and maturity.

I am so proud of the young man you have become and know that you have a future in helping young people deal with loss. I feel like you have found your calling. From our brief meeting, I can tell where your heart is.

Your passion is getting this message out to others like you. You are going to make a difference in the lives that cross your path. I'm so excited for you, Xavier. So excited that we have discovered a passion of yours.

Remember when I said, "Imagine going to school for something you are truly interested in and reading about philosophies that you are truly interested in?"

You responded with "I know, right? What a difference that makes." Well, you have found it, and let's get you started.

Thank you Xavier and Briana for sharing your dad and your story with the world. Somewhere out there, people will identify with your story and inevitably be changed because of your courage to share.

I adore you both, and I can't wait to see the GOOD that you generate from following your passion.

Much love,

Ms. Romero

# 12

# KILLED FOR THE GREATER GOOD

I'M ORAS, A thirteen-year-old Assyrian. My story is unusual as I was born and raised in Iraq, but moved to Lebanon after my father died. I am the middle child of brothers, and we all came to the United States in 2009 when I was in the fourth grade.

In Lebanan, I attended boarding school, which I loved because we would attend school, go to parks, and play a lot. It was just like the Harry Potter movies. They would serve us meals on the big, long tables, and we would sleep there too. I loved my time there. On the weekends though, I would return home and spend time with my mom and my brothers.

Here in America, life is different. I learned to play American football, and I play left tackle, even though I would love to play wide receiver. I also love dogs, and I have a puppy pitbull named Rex. I love him because he has really soft skin under his chin, and he is my best friend. I am the only person that walks and runs with him, cleans his poop, and plays with him. In school, I love working hard, and I really want a college degree so I can grow up to be whatever I want. At home, I love the television show *Pitbulls and Paroles* as well as *The Walking Dead*. I love all types of music, but my favorite is Eminem's "I'm Not Afraid." I truly consider myself a normal kid except for the fact that I lost my father, Waad, in 2006 when he was killed by a roadside bomb in Baghdad, Iraq.

Waad had hazel eyes and loved to play fight with us. We all used to jump on him, and he would pick us all up at the same time. We hung onto his arms like monkeys. My father was a great man. He was the type of person that you wanted to tell everything to. However, if you did a bad thing in front of him, you were punished with a water hose.

My father would have been thirty-eight this year. He liked soccer, and he would hang out at the soccer stadium a lot. In fact, we would have soccer games with all the moms against the dads and/or the kids against the parents. Those games were really fun, and I miss our times together.

For his career, dad used to work in the military for the United States as an Iraqi citizen. He would build safe houses for the American soldiers and would lay blocks to protect the Americans in the trenches. He fought alongside the Americans. I remember he had an AK-47, and he would take it with him when he would leave the house.

The day I found out my dad died, it was on a day that my mom was making butter at my aunt's house. We returned home and noticed the sidewalks were packed with cars. I thought it was a party, but when we went inside my grandma's garage, I saw everyone crying. My grandma, uncle, my aunt, my entire family was there.

My grandma pulled my mother aside and told her. Instantly my mother dropped to the ground and started crying. I thought that my grandpa died, but it wasn't my grandpa. Grandpa was there. Everyone was there—except for my dad.

When it clicked inside my head, I felt like the world dropped onto my shoulders. It was an out of body experience–time slowed down. I cried. I tried not to show it much, and ultimately, I went upstairs and tried to act like nothing. I didn't want people knowing that I cry. My brothers were crying also, but they were downstairs though. I was the only one that came upstairs.

Mom came upstairs and said, "Oras, we are going to be alone for a few years." I didn't say anything. I was stunned.

Before the funeral, the only persons to see him in his coffin were my older brother and my mom. I was too young.

At the funeral, everybody around me was crying. I just stood there and not a tear fell. I don't know why. It just didn't feel right to cry. I really tried to cry, but no tears would come out. I was broken inside. I hurt like someone was stomping on me so hard. It was a constant pain.

During the ceremony, the person who got up to speak was crying so intensely, I couldn't understand them. No music, just people crying. There was a picture of my dad hung up over his coffin. There was praying by the priest from the Bible and everyone else was crying. It was a Catholic service.

At the burial site in Baghdad, there were other fresh graves there also, some brand-new and some old. Family and friends stood over his burial spot and spoke about him and what a wonderful man he was. His American friends, who showed up in uniform, shook my hand and hugged me. The ceremony ended and people threw their flowers on top of him.

When we returned home, everyone sat in their spot and was quiet. No one said anything. There was food, but no one ate. No one ate for four or five days. The kids were fed, but all the adults did not. There were so upset that they didn't eat.

Over time, my grandma would make me coffee and talk with me. We would sit on the front porch and talk about the weather and find clouds that were in shapes of different animals and objects. It was just us, our alone time. We were the early birds. It was our only time together because during the rest of the day, the family was there. It was nice to have conversation time with her that wasn't about the loss of my father.

My mom cried a lot, for weeks afterwards, and I really felt bad for her. We all lived together for a while, my extended family. Three years later, mom found a house and she started working as a housecleaner.

It took me about four years to forget or to at least stop thinking that my father was going to come home. My mom wore black clothes for seven years. It's a ritual in my culture. You must wear dark clothes for seven years, and she wore it for seven years. Seeing her dressed in black all the time did not help me in forgetting the situation. However, I understand the concept and she was honoring him.

I believe my dad has come back in spirit, and it makes me very happy. One day we were in Lebanon, and it was around three in the morning and I woke up to use the bathroom. I was inside with the door open when a shadow walked by. It was a dark shadow. I thought it was one of my brothers, but when I returned to the room they were both fast asleep and hadn't moved an inch. I didn't know what to think.

But later on a few weeks later, my brothers and I were camping on the roof, and there was only one light up there. Again, I woke up and saw a shadow walking. I also heard my mom downstairs talking to somebody as I saw a shadow move across the wall. It's crazy though. I felt no fear when I saw the shadow.

My house was two stories and when I saw that shadow, I knew it was my dad visiting me. I felt it. The very same day, I went into my room and immediately my eyes went to a picture of my father on the wall. I just knew. My eyes had never just gone to that picture. It was out of my control how it happened. I was really excited though because I knew he was watching over me. I never shared this incident with anyone. In fact, I have never spoken to anyone about my dad's death, not my friends or my brothers. I have not spoken to anyone until now, and it feels good to share this with you.

Another time that I felt my dad was near was when I was looking in my wallet for some money. It just so happened to be on his birthday when his picture accidently fell out. It was a picture of my dad wearing a dark green button-up shirt. On the back of it, my name, my bro's name, and my other bro's name were written on it. His picture never falls out. It was tucked away in a section where plastic sticks to it, and it never falls out. It happened about a year and a half ago, and I smiled really big. On my insides, I felt excitement. Still don't understand how that picture fell out. It had to be him. Spirit works in mysterious ways.

At night when no one can see me, I pray and I talk to my dad. I will never forget him nor will my mother. My mom reads the Bible on his birthday and wears the black bandana over her head in honor of him.

How I dealt with losing my dad was by not talking about it with anybody. It felt more comfortable with people not knowing. I didn't want to be viewed as different or having people feel sorry for me. So it was easier for me or so I thought.

Well, since I'm writing this it actually feels good to be talking about this with somebody for the first time. I can finally get it out of my system. I feel a weight lifted off of me. I feel better now knowing that someone knows and understands me. At first I was unsure if I wanted to share my story, but now that it's out, I wish I shared it earlier. I wish I opened up earlier. I feel so much better now.

If you are going through this or are about to go through this, don't worry cause everything will turn out better for you in the future. You will have a lot more confidence to share if you have a teacher like mine. Yes, your loss will hurt, and it will continue to hurt. But in time, you'll be ready to share it with others going through the same experience as you.

If I could offer any advice, I am telling you to go on with your life, and your parent or loved one will visit you whenever you are ready. They know when you are ready. Just be open to it. Just keep doing what's on your mind, and don't be afraid of anything because there is someone up there truly protecting you.

---

Dear Dad,

If I had one chance to tell you what I've missed about you while you were gone, I would tell you this. I've missed how you used to come back home from your job and even when you were tired, you didn't show it because you didn't want us to be sad and think you were tired of playing with us. I will also never forget how you always gave me a kiss on my cheek when you used to come back home from work and your beard used to tickle me always. Also, how you used to show off your muscles to mom by trying to pick up my brothers and me at the same time.

These are the things I've missed while you're gone, and I will try very hard to be the great man that you were. Thanks for all the things you've taught me.

I LOVE YOU!

Oras

---

My dearest Oras,

Boy, am I glad that we connected, and from what you've written, I think you are too.

There is no doubt in my mind that your daddy is with you, checking on you, and making sure that the loves of his life are safe.

He is a hero in every sense of the word. He sacrificed his life to help others defeat an oppressive regime. He helped save the lives of many soldiers worldwide who took part in that fight and for that, I am very appreciative of who your father was and appreciate what he did for others. He risked his time with you and your family, in essence his life, to help a cause that he believed in strongly; he was a crusader of sorts. He put others' needs before his own by putting himself in harm's way, and that is admirable. He was a courageous and strong-willed man, and I see those characteristics in you.

I'm so glad that you finally spoke to someone about your loss, and I am honored that it was me. No one should have to shoulder that burden like you have been doing for years. By telling your story, you are honoring this great man and healing yourself, too.

He is so proud of you. I feel it. I believe it with every ounce of my being. Continue to make him proud. Live your life for him like he would want you to live. That is the greatest gift you could give him, by living the best life. Do and accomplish what he would have wanted, and as you're achieving different milestones throughout your life, look above and say, "This one is for you, Dad." He is watching, Oras. He is with you.

Thank you, Oras, for being you, so kind, sweet, and sensitive. You're strength is admirable, and sharing your story with the world just magnifies your greatness.

"There are things we don't want to happen but have to accept, things we don't want to know but have to learn, and people we can't live without but have to let go." Unknown

*The above saying is profound, but the word "temporarily" needs to be added to the end of it. Your loss is temporary, Oras, and you will be reunited with your father's soul again when you cross and in future lifetimes. Truth.*

*Ain't got nothing but love for you, Sweetie! :)*

*Ms. Romero*

# 13

# LIVIN' ON THE WILD SIDE

I'M JAY DIAZ and my brother Bruno Guillermo Diaz was one of the most tough, laid back, and "chill" human beings that I've ever known. I use to feel like there was nobody that quite understood me inside and out, but Bruno was the exception.

I knew his every weakness and strength. Bruno was always random and a fun presence to have around. Throughout our childhood, we always competed at who was better at something. Later on, we established that he was the better looking, and I was the smarter one. He always seemed surprised at my knowledge, and I was surprised at how he lived.

Bruno grabbed life by the throat and lived it to the fullest. He did so many crazy things—he called it an "adventure." Many people knew him as that funny guy because he was always making jokes. I knew him differently.

I knew him as the only human on this Earth that loved me, generally looked like me, and understood me. We were either confused as twins or people thought I was him.

One thing I will never forget are our conversations we had about the future. What we will do after high school, and were we going to start a family? Once he asked the hardest question that I couldn't answer. He asked, "Have you ever thought which one of us will get married first?"

I looked at him and said, "I don't know really. I suck at love, whether I find someone now or probably at college, only time will tell."

Those were the type of memorable moments I had with him.

A month before he died, it was my 18th birthday. He came into my room and said, "Finally 18… Happy Birthday, Man."

Bruno was an amazing, caring person who loved family, friendship, and life. When my brother died, I was sleeping. It was his birthday, July 8, 2013. He died around 4:35 a.m. riding his bike home from a friend's house. He had no reflectors and was struck from behind by a Jeep and killed on impact.

I woke up that morning thinking I had a training session with my personal trainer at my gym. When I went into the kitchen and served myself cereal, I saw his bedroom door open. A strange feeling came over me. It was unreal—a feeling I've never felt before. I felt separated from the world for a good minute.

I looked at the time and saw that I was running late. I made it to the gym and it turned out that I didn't have any sessions until tomorrow. So, I just worked out until I received a call from the County Sheriff.

He said he wanted to look for my mom claiming they'd found her phone. The problem was that she didn't have a phone. I told them where I lived anyway, so they could drop it off with my niece since she was home.

My niece then called me and told me the cops were looking for my mother. So I asked, "Did they leave a phone there?"

She replied, "No."

That's when I started feeling strange again. I called the Sheriff's Department again, and they wanted to speak with my mom. I immediately ended the workout and ran home. Once I arrived, my niece was scared, and we waited for my mom.

When my mom arrived home, I told her the police were looking for her and she got worried that something might have happened to Bruno.

Twenty minutes later, two men came knocking. It was a detective with the last name Machado and a translator. We allowed them inside, and he told us that a bicyclist was hit and died on the scene with no identification. They needed us to identify him.

I felt the hair rise on the back of my neck. I was questioning how does this tie into Bruno? What did he do? There was a part of me that wanted to know and a part of me that didn't want to know. My curiosity kept going nonetheless.

So I asked, "Is the bicyclist Bruno?"

I prayed and hoped that it wasn't Bruno, but when he opened his folder, he pulled out a picture of a person with no life. And sure enough, it was my brother Bruno. He looked asleep with jaw slightly open and a couple red spots on his face that were probably bruises. He looked asleep but this time, unfortunately, he wasn't going to wake up.

I tried to find a way of saying that it wasn't him, but I couldn't. My mother saw it at the same time and said along with me, "Yes, that's him."

Tears followed immediately, and we lost our minds. My niece broke down sobbing, and my mother was devastated. She grabbed her chest like it was ripped apart from her, clutching her neck. Me with no control of myself and filled with rage yelled, "He's no longer with us????????????? It was his BIRTHDAY!!!!!"

The cop just nodded.

My brother died on his 17th birthday.

I felt a whole HUGE chunk of me died when I learned of my brother's death. I just wanted to leave, fly. My whole world had just collapsed permanently into a world of sorrow without mercy.

It changed me into an indescribable person. I felt like a scientist needed to bring me back into reality like Frankenstein. I literally felt split apart and the other half just left me. Sometimes I look into the mirror and I see Bruno looking back at me. I feel honored. We were black and white, yin and yang. We were so different, yet so much alike. We both wanted a good life.

But, amidst all this, Detective Machado told me to be strong for everyone, and from that moment, a new feeling came over me. I felt he was speaking for someone else, whether it was spirit or God, this soulless messenger seemed to have a soul. The feeling gave me a new purpose and turned me into a being that wasn't scared—merciless to any challenge.

I arranged the funeral with help. I felt fortunate. I was grateful that he was dressed as a military soldier going into rest. That's who he was when he was alive, a soldier of God, fighting for a purpose, and he did.

Sometimes I question his death, but what's the point? God needed him.

My brother's girlfriend's mom said that he served his purpose. While we were at his fundraising car wash, Tyanna saw two boys riding their bikes and asked, how come they weren't dying and how come it was Bruno? Her mom told her that those boys have a different destiny and their own lessons to teach those who love them when they cross over.

Seeing everyone wearing white and camo at his funeral was honorable and his essence filled the church. I felt love despite my anger. But needless to say, the love in the room was there, and I felt tremendous support.

To see my brother's coffin, I wasn't sure if he was really dead. I wanted to know if that was a different person. I was in disbelief. I ignored all symptoms of grieving, and frankly, I'm still ignoring them.

Seeing my brother, my little brother in that coffin was extremely devastating. So awful, that I didn't want anyone touching me. His body was cold, and it didn't feel like him. His presence wasn't in his body. He was with God, and now I firmly believe, he is my Guardian Angel.

The funeral was my saying goodbye to him on Earth for now.

Since his passing, Bruno has visited me three times in my dreams. The first time, I dreamt I was in my living room with Rachel who is like my cousin. She was smiling at me and he was sitting behind her in his red boxers. Then he started to fade away from his toes to all of his body. That's when I screamed, "Don't! Stop reminding me of what I don't have!"

What followed was that I felt a sensation like I was falling, and I woke up crying. I felt it was a visiting hour of sorts and my falling sensation was myself falling back down to Earth.

I get so jealous of seeing others with their brothers because having a brother is the best thing in the world. They are always there for you, or so I thought he would be. They are the best friend who knows you, who you are, and how hard life is for you and your family. Who else other than your very own brother?

In the second dream visit, I was playing with him in our backyard from our previous house, and he was swinging on the swing. We both loved that swing. It was the best thing about that house until he broke it one day. In my dream he was swinging, smiling, and laughing and said, "Hey, Jose, watch this!"

My brother was happy and jumped off the swing and flew away into the sky. I believe he was revisiting our childhood times together with me and his flying away was himself leaving the visit.

The third time he came, I dreamt that my mom knew about the death of him and told me, "Your brother's dead."

In my dream I woke up and his body was next to me. I was then teleported to where he got hit, and I saw my mom dragging his body crying and screaming at the sky. To my right shoulder, Bruno was there and started talking to me. He said, "I know you guys miss me, but don't worry."

I responded crying, "I miss you a lot."

Our conversation felt like an eternity, but I couldn't remember the exact things he said and/or what I said. However, I do remember him saying one thing before I woke up. He said, "You need to start thinking of what's more important in this world—take care of mom."

So, in light of the current turmoil going on in my household, I find my brother's words speaking to me in how I deal with my father now, about his treatment of my mom and me. My mother is my greatest influence. She is my role model and my new best friend. She is a priority in my life and my independence in the future is going to impact her greatly. However she told me one day, "Wherever you're at in your life, Mijo… if you're happy, then I'm happy."

Another way I connect with my brother is through music. Songs remind me of my brother and I'm instantly reminded of him when I hear them. "Three Little Birds" by Bob Marley reminds me of his personality. "Pursuit of Happiness" by Kid Cudi reminds me of his life and how it ended. Whereas, Justin Timberlake's "Mirrors" reminds me of our childhood, brotherhood, and how we were always thought of as twins. In fact, we were both referred to as the "Twin Towers" because we were so tall. One last song is Tyga's "Far Away" which he once dedicated to his girlfriend. Their special relationship had a lot of ups and downs, and that song describes how he felt towards her—how he messed up so many times, and how he can't live without her.

I receive signs of him being around me quite a lot. I can smell the scent of his flowers and his skin from the funeral at times. Even more strange is that we have lamps in the house that only turn on by touch. The lamps are decorated in the Virgin Mary Guadalupe. Well, these lights turn on in his room and in my room by themselves.

One day when this happened, I had experienced a horrible day. I was kept from taking my SAT's that would have allowed me to potentially get into a dream school for college. When the proctors turned me away, I felt defeated and as if my future was ruined.

So, I arrived at home, and I was super down. I noticed something glowing outside my brother's window, and I was like what and the hell is that? I was praying that it would be him in his room because the lights were on, the lights that can only be turned on by TOUCH. No one was home though, my parents were with me, and the lamp was on in his room.

I went to my room and the lamp was on also in there. I told my parents, and they said that it was a sign that he visited us. He came when I was at a super low point in my life. That visit made me feel hopeful because I felt that I wasn't alone. Bruno had messed up plenty of times, and the message I received was that I can mess up and still pick myself up and keep on fighting.

My most recent visit occurred during a marathon. Yes, a marathon. Since his death, I had decided to train and run a marathon. Well, being a busy teenage boy I didn't train very well, but I attempted the race anyway. As I suffered into the second half of the race, I smelled my brother's scent. The marathon—as you can imagine—was brutal, but I felt he was there alongside me. I smelled him, most strongly when I wanted to give up, and I firmly believe that he got me through the race.

Accomplishing that marathon pushed my limits and I survived. I couldn't stop smiling for a week afterward. I still can't believe that I decided to run one and more importantly, that I finished it. No doubt that my brother helped me with that one.

We have honored him since his death. One month after Bruno died on the first day of school, we released fifteen balloons to symbolize his class year 2015. Additionally to this day, I continue to wear his tribute shirt and post pictures at least once a month on Instagram from either the past or from his burial.

If I knew this was coming and that I was going to lose my brother, I would have wanted to know the loss of friendships that would result because of my brother's death. It would have helped me forget or at least cope with the pain more effectively. Some people simply can't handle being around me because they don't know what to say and it makes things awkward. Others are so self-absorbed, especially at my age, that it makes dealing with loss more difficult. Some disappeared, some were there, and some just couldn't handle it.

I'd change a lot of things about this event if I could. I would really love to go back in time to wish him a happy birthday. If I could have only caught him sneaking out that night and told him to stay home instead. I would have given him whatever he wanted if he would have just stayed.

My advice to others reading this would be to "Live your life like you're going to die young, seize the moment, learn like you're going to live forever, and rethink any risky situations. Also, grab any good opportunity you have been given by the throat. I'm going to end with this. I'm not going to tell you everything is going to be okay because I would be a hypocrite. I can only hope with time that it gets better."

I read on twitter a story about a British psychologist that really hit home with me. He was talking about a cup of water. He said something along the lines of "If I hold this cup for hours, my hand will be weak. If I hold it for a day, I will ache. My hand will get tired, but nothing happens to the water. It's still there, and I'm still holding it. But sometimes, we just need to put down the cup and let it go." Think about that one. Makes sense.

I can't let it go though, for now. Hopefully, some day I can. I would also tell you to expect to feel this feeling for a while and to do what makes you happy, that is, if you can function. I couldn't function for a while at school and in life, but I'm working on it.

When Bruno was alive and I would get frustrated, he would tell me every time, "Niggah, niggah, chill."

So, that's my advice for everyone. Chill... and love life.

---

*Dear Bruno,*

*It's been six months already since you've gone to be with God. Wow...it seems like a lifetime since we talked or made fun of each other. I would give anything to hear your voice or even better, to have you around. I miss everything about you...your smile, your laugh, and even when you take my shirt, hat, and/or jeans.*

*Times are so hard—you don't want to know. I shed and have witnessed tears, ENOUGH tears to create an ocean. Seeing Mom and Dad cry is the most painful thing ever. Mom and Dad are so torn up and so are your friends, especially the love of your life Tyanna. What a mess this has become!*

There isn't a day that I don't think of you and the memories we had together. Thank you for being there for me with my struggles and in reminding me who I am, not who I should be. I feel honored to have known such an awesome human being.

Things are extremely different, and I'm fighting for the pursuit of happiness in hope that someday we will see each other again. Seeing you rise above and knowing you're in paradise with God makes me feel more secure.

Thank you for all the memories, Bruno. Keep watching and continue to protect us. I want more visits. I am in desperate need of a visit, my brother. Hook me up!

I love you.

> Always,
> Chemaso

---

Dearest Jay,

Your wound is very fresh and your strength is admirable. You've undergone a tremendous year, and hopefully being a part of this book project has helped you.

I love that Bruno has made his presence known to you. Those are gifts, my dear. Your willingness to receive them is a sure sign that you will receive more.

Live your life with him in mind. Continue to set goals for yourself and work towards them. He is with you and will relish in all your accomplishments as he did with the marathon.

Jay, I want you to focus on living in the present and loving the present moment. Thich Nhat Hanh, one of the most respected Buddhist Zen Masters today, says it well, and if you concentrate on its meaning, it can help your quality of life that you're currently experiencing. Really think about this, my dear.

"Life can be found only in the present moment. The past is gone, the future is not yet here, and if we do not go back to ourselves in the present moment, we cannot be in touch with life."

The following by Lao Tzu is also profound and clarifies it further.

"If you are depressed you are living in the past.
If you are anxious you are living in the future.
If you are at peace you are living in the present."

You may not get tomorrow, Jay, so please enjoy today. Unfortunately, you learned that the hard way. Please ensure sure that your moments are happy, and only you can make yourself happy.

I know you, Jay, and right now you're saying, "But how do I get happy?" Dale Carnegie says it well,

"It isn't what you have, or who you are, or where you are,
or what you are doing that makes you happy or unhappy.
It is what you think about."

Take that. Bam! Only you can make yourself happy. It's what you think about.

I want only the best for you, Jay. You're a wonderful human being, and I'm certain that you have a bright future ahead.

Stay in the present, and be grateful for what you have. Gratitude is key, and it will open your heart and help rewire your brain.

Keep in touch, and if you ever need someone to listen, I am here for you.

Sincerely,
Ms. Romero

# 14

## STILL NOT OVER IT, BUT I HAVE REASON TO SMILE AGAIN

I KNEW ONE day that it would happen. My parents would grow old and die. I surely never wanted to have to write about it, especially being so young. But this is how it goes, I guess.

If I could do anything to rewind back time, I would. Suicide is one thing, but losing a parent is another. I was thirteen when my dad took his own life.

My dad Michael was thirty-one, and my mother named me Michaela after him. I am the spitting image of my father, and all throughout my childhood, I wanted to be just like him. Actually, I was a daddy's girl, and the reality is that I still am.

My dad was incredibly smart and ever so handsome. Growing up until the day he died, he was into physical fitness. He used to be a body-builder model for local fitness magazines. If there were three words to describe my dad as I knew him, they would be self-less, educated, and determined.

I always remember my dad being in school. He worked two jobs at the age of 17 to support me. He started at MJC and transferred to Stanislaus State University where he graduated. In fact, all throughout my childhood, he worked two jobs and went to school to create a better future for himself and his family.

My dad was my *everything*—the one person in the world who stayed consistent in my life and the one person who always looked out for me. So when I woke up, August 23, 2007, my life took a real twist—one I wasn't prepared for.

I remember waking up suddenly due to the loud noise and seeing the time from my alarm clock projected on the ceiling. It was 8:15. I was supposed to be babysitting my sister that day. The whole week prior my dad couldn't sleep. He was on his third day with no sleep when he checked into the hospital. He talked to a psychiatrist and was given medication to help him sleep.

My dad was never one to take pills. He said growing up as a kid, his mind would play tricks on him when he took certain medications, and it was going to be the same case this time around.

At this point in time of his career, my dad worked as the head accountant for a big company in San Ramon, California. The stress from work took a toll on his sleep. When the doctor put him on medication to help him, he went delusional.

My dad never showed his disturbed emotions to my little sister or me. He kept to himself with personal issues.

But at one point two days before he died, he wrote to my aunt. In his email he told her he was put on medication to sleep and his mind was racing a mile per minute. He felt like he wasn't doing his job as a husband and father. He felt like he wasn't good for anybody and that he had let us all down. He also said he was having nightmares where he was killing himself, and he asked my aunt to come see him as soon as possible. Unfortunately, she was too late.

So back to that awful morning, I saw the time on the clock and thought to myself it was way too early to be awake. My dad was going back to work, and my step mom got a new job so I agreed to watch over my little sister. I remember waking. I got up out of bed for a glass of water and went back to sleep. When I ultimately woke up, I went about my day with my sister playing games around the house. I had no idea what was about to happen.

Around 11 o'clock, my stepmom showed up at the apartment and asked, "Where is your father?"

Apparently, his car was parked out front, but there was no sign of him anywhere.

I replied, "I don't know. I haven't heard from him all day."

She looked worried. She immediately went back to their bedroom only to find that the door was locked. She told me to go to the apartment office and get a key to open the door, so I did.

When I came back she went in the bedroom, and I returned to the kitchen with my sister. I thought nothing of it. I had Disney on in the background, and I was coloring with my sis having a good time.

My stepmom went inside the room for roughly 5-10 minutes.

When my step mom came out, her green eyes were like the size of quarters. They were huge. She was on the phone with the police department telling them she had a 13-year-old and a 6-year-old daughter, and she turned and went back into the bedroom. She was in a total state of shock.

I remember I went outside with my sister to color. We put a maple leaf under a paper, and shaded them into silhouettes of the leaves. We came back inside and I popped open two gogurts for us.

As we sat down to eat, the police busted through the house. They didn't knock. Some went towards my dad's room. Two officers in the main room turned off the TV and told me that I had to leave with my sister. I still had no idea at this point. I had never seen so many cops. There were three or four cop cars, two fire trucks, and an ambulance. My mind was thinking every possible thought. I thought a homeless person broke into the room and fell asleep. I didn't know. I really had no idea. I thought of everything, but my dad. I just thought he was MIA at the gym or something while all this craziness was happening.

My step mom, however, was in the bedroom the entire time.

Outside, I was met by another police officer. I stood on the stairs and watched as more cars arrived and emergency vehicles. The last to arrive was the ambulance, and I remember feeling upset. I was upset because if he was hurt, shouldn't they be hurrying? Why weren't they there sooner?

I turned to the cop and asked, "What is going on? Do you know? Have you heard? Can you find out?"

He replied that he didn't know and that he received a call to be with us, and that was it. He simply kept to himself. He didn't comfort us at all. Another cop was more soothing. He said that a manager would let us into an empty apartment next to our current building.

CPS was the next to arrive after we waited 10-15 minutes more. CPS is Child Protective Services. The agent was in her mid-thirties. She was nice. She held both our hands and took us on a walk.

So I asked her, "What is going on?"

That is when another lady came and took my little sister.

The first lady then told me that my dad had passed away. I didn't believe it. It was like "No, you don't know what you're talking about." My brain wasn't going to take it as a reality because it wouldn't happen, and it couldn't happen. When I gathered up enough courage to ask how, she told me that he shot himself. She looked very sad, and I don't remember how I felt.

My memory jumps to when I'm back in the holding house with the police officers. CPS left and the police officers were not comforting at all. My sister was never told. She was still gone. I tried to escape and jump off the balcony because I felt that if I could be in there, I could save his life. Or maybe if it were a nightmare, I would wake up.

Five minutes later my stepmom came in, and she looked as if she had been crying. She held me and we cried together. She asked me what she was going to do and how or if she was going to tell my sister what had happened. She told me to be strong for my sister, and that my family was coming shortly.

My stepmom left me with a cop who told me that he was going back inside the apartment and asked me if there was anything I wanted because they were not going to let me back inside.

I told him that I wanted the sweater my dad let me use the night before and for some pictures of him. I remember saying please.

From the apartment, we were taken to a police car where we waited fifteen minutes until the cop returned with the pictures and the sweater.

They brought me two pictures of my dad, one of which I gave to my sister. My sister returned to the apartment while the police officer was gone, and I cried and held her. She was crying too, and she didn't know why she was sad. They told her that daddy was sick. I'm not sure if she knows that her dad committed suicide. Even to this day.

They took my sister and I to a hotel where we sat on the patio/porch and walked around. They tried to buy us whatever we wanted from the food shop. I clearly didn't want anything. I was just so upset.

Family started showing up at the hotel, and I just sat there and cried. I didn't want to talk to anybody. I wanted to be left alone. My real mom never even showed up to come and get me. I felt awful. I had never experienced the feeling of losing somebody to whom there was no possibility of them coming back. My dad was literally ripped right out of my life and I had no say or part in stopping it.

The family members that arrived were very sad. Some were crying. I was uncomfortable. If I was talking, I felt like I should be crying. If I was crying, I felt like I should be talking. It was just the biggest shock ever. I just kept trying to wake myself up. I kept wishing I were in a coma. I was thinking they were going to say surprise, just kidding, or this was all a big joke. That message never came.

My sister went with my step grandma, I think, and I went with my grandparents to their house in Cupertino, my biological mother's parents. I couldn't concentrate. I couldn't sleep. My aunts came and stayed with me and I really didn't know how to deal with the pain. One moment I was fine, then I felt guilty for feeling fine. Then, I'd be crying the next minute—it was a rollercoaster of emotions. I kept waking up. I felt guilty about being asleep. How could I sleep on the night my dad died?

Nothing was okay.

I really can't put it into words how one reacts when they hear those words. Crying wasn't even enough. I wanted to barf up my insides and tear my skin off. I was so upset. I still am.

My grandparents had worked the next day and I was bounced to the next house—my aunt and uncle's in Livermore, my mom's brother and wife. They tried to keep my mind off the pain, but his death was the only thing I could think of. My uncle was a tall, slender guy with a really big heart. He is exceptionally smart and reminded me of my dad, which made it hard to be around him. My uncle, aunt, and my little cousin Paige tried to do activities with me to keep my mind off of the experience.

Of course, nothing could distract me from all the mixed emotions running through my body. I remember them taking me to a sandy beach. It happened to be the same cozy beach my father took me to a week before he died.

As my toes sunk into the sand, I began to cry. For just the week earlier, I was burying my dad in the sand under my feet where he laid warm and full of life.

In a couple of days, I would be burying my dad in a coffin under the earth, where he lay cold and absent from his body. It was as if all time stood still. Nothing mattered except the fact that my daddy was gone forever—and that he was not coming back.

School was about to start, and after two days with my aunt and uncle, they took me to Modesto to be with my biological mother. I went to my room in her house and stared at every single crack in the wall and tried to think of every memory that I could. I relived the situation over and over in my mind. I played eeenie, meeny, miney, mo, with myself on whether I was going to kill myself or not. I couldn't handle the pain, and I just wanted to be with him. I wanted to be with my dad.

I never left my room unless I was going to my grandma's house (my dad's mother). At her house, I would go and look at photos of my dad, some which were with my step-mom, other family members, and myself. My face would turn red and it felt hot like someone was holding a lighter to my cheek and the flame was burning it. Tears would begin to build in my eyes like big water bombs waiting to escape from my eyelids.

My family was broken. Who would walk me down the aisle when I got married? My kids would never know their grandpa. My husband would never know the greatest person in my life. My heart pounded as I began to think about all of the things my dad would not be there for: middle school graduation, high school graduation, college graduation, me getting my first job, teaching me how to drive, becoming an adult, and every Father's day.

Everything was ruined. I needed him. He let my sister down, he let my mom down—he let me down. No one saw it coming. My dad was not the kind of person to share his emotions with others. He was strong and independent. He kept to himself. He had even questioned the idea of people committing suicide like it was something he would never understand and NEVER do.

School started four days after his death, and I was an emotional disaster. Never would I have thought my life would put me through this. It was my 8th grade year, and I did not want to be there. I wore sunglasses, and I left class a lot. Kids even accused me of lying and claimed that I just wanted attention. Really?

I did actually end up trying to commit suicide twice. Losing my dad had led me into a depression that I had never felt before. I never knew what it was like to not have a choice or a say in losing someone I love so dearly. I felt suicide for myself was the way to be with my dad again.

Who was to know if he'd go to Heaven or Hell, or if he'd be stuck in between? According to a church in Modesto, he would go to Hell. This scared me. But then I thought if I just did it too, I would be sure to end up wherever he was, and it couldn't be Hell. It just couldn't be Hell because my dad was too good of a man to go to Hell over something his brain had no control over.

The second time I tried, I went through with everything, and it didn't work. I overdosed on a methylphenidate like Adderall. I took seven pills because I knew of someone else who did, and it put them in a coma where they just woke up last year.

My aunt and uncle tried to get me to throw up the pills. They stuck a stick down my throat and took me to the emergency room since I couldn't throw it up. The hospital said, "Don't let her sleep for 24 hours." I was completely numb from head to toe, my jaw was locked, and I was veritably tired. They didn't pump me. They just let it work through my system, since there was nothing else that they could do.

Since his crossing, my dad has come to me in my dreams, through symbols and through mysterious phone calls. Three days after my father died, I was getting a lecture from my grandmother to get off of my phone and to get my stuff done. School was starting, and she wanted me to get rest. That is when my cell phone rang. I was texting when I heard this strange ringtone that was not my ringtone. It was the sound of an old school house phone with NO breaks in the extra long ring. The ring rang three minutes, ongoing, non-stop. I removed the battery, and it kept going. There was an untraceable number on the screen. Not restricted, not private, it was just strange. Even stranger... when I turned my phone back on, there was no record of the phone call on my phone whatsoever.

I knew it was *him* immediately. I had the gut feeling that it was my dad. He wanted me to go to sleep, get off the phone, and listen to my grandmother. I was excited, and it gave me insight that my dad was still around, that I wasn't alone, and that he was just a thought away.

The second phone call occurred when I was a sophomore in high school. We were hanging out at the canal. The ring tone my dad had before his death went off on my cell phone. "Morris Brown" by Outcast. He loved that song.

That was NOT my cell phone ring tone. Again, the call was "untraceable." It just kept ringing/playing. The phone would not let me answer the phone. It would not switch over. We took the battery out and put it back in. The song finally stopped and my entire phone shut down. When I turned it back on, the call was not on the call log.

My dad was definitely trying to contact me. I was so happy and relieved that he still watches over me.

In a way it sucks that he was taken from me without any notice. But what also sucks is knowledge that you're going to lose your parent. I empathize with those of you suffering that way. Having to arrange those last weeks and days would have been difficult to say the least. I wouldn't know what to say looking death in its eye, knowing it's going to take someone I love. I would have simply spent every last second of time possible with him. My situation was different regretfully. Had I known he was going to commit suicide—I could have stopped him. I would have stopped him.

I go to his gravesite every birthday. I talk to him before every big event such as tests, exams, life-threatening situations like when I'm in a car with a crazy driver, an interview—or something scary like cliff jumping into a river. I find myself saying, "I'll do it for you, Daddy."

Whenever I need to push myself to the limit, I think of my dad asking me, "Will you do it for me?"

Guess what? I do it.

I don't have any advice for getting over it because I'm still not over it. I have nightmares sometimes. I had a dream last night that I was committing suicide a million different ways, and I could never do it. I would never die, and eventually, I woke up. I also see people once in a while that look like him, that resemble him, and it freaks me out. But I'm sure that is normal.

On a brighter note, I am exceedingly thankful to have had my family surrounding me to make sure that I was okay. Without them keeping their eyes on me at this time, I may not be here today. Family is meant to be there when times are hard as well as when times are good.

My dad's situation is a perfect example of why it's important that if help is needed, to ask for it. It is okay to reach out to others. Going through this, I turned to friends and family to keep me sane. During this horrible event, I needed them the most and they were there for me. I am blessed. I am alive, and as for today, I am smiling, and you will smile again too.

---

*Dear Dad,*

*I would give anything and everything... I would give every last breath of air I have to bring you back, just so I could hug you once more, hold your hand once more, just to see you once more. Everyday I miss you and wish that I could go back in time and stop you from making the choice that you did.*

*Our memories are fading, and it hurts me to know that one day I may hardly remember them at all. Holidays are coming up. I'm thinking this year I'm going to try and put a smile on my face.*

*I usually do, but there are always those few minutes where I separate myself from my surroundings and cry a little. Don't worry though. It's not as bad as it used to be. I feel as IF I shed a few tears for you, it would pour down rain in Heaven, and you'd definitely know that your daughter is thinking of you.*

*That is, if you are in Heaven. I tried going to church to help give me some guidance, but the Pastor kept preaching that those who take their* own life go to Hell. You don't belong in Hell, Daddy. I couldn't even see you in jail because you always set a good example for my sister and me.

It's unfortunate that I don't have many photos of you and almost nothing that you left behind. My memories of us are almost all I have left and there is NOT ONE day that goes by where I'm not reminded of you.

You worked harder than anyone I've ever known to support me. Now, I have my own son to care for and look after. It's almost been 7 years, and it feels like it just happened.

One minute you were telling me goodnight, and the next morning you were gone. No goodbye. No note. Nothing. Nobody is or was there to protect me. Nobody was there to raise me. When you died, I had me and myself only. I see how differently my life could have been had you chosen to stay in it. It has taught me to never walk out on those you love.

I wish nothing more than for you to be here, to hold and love Haiden, and to look at him the same way that you used to look at me. I love and miss you, Dad.

Forever missing you,

Emmy

———

Emmy dear,

We were certainly destined to meet. No question in my mind. You were given to me literally days after your daddy crossed over.

I certainly empathize with what you've had to deal with in your short lifetime. Your story is so heartfelt and brutally raw. As I listen to you relive your tragedy, I am in awe of your strength and candor. I'm so glad to be in your life, and I consider you a daughter of mine.

I have seen you grow up into a beautiful young lady. You have such a generous heart——you would give the shirt off of your back to anyone in need. I have witnessed you in action, and you are ever so kind to anyone. You adopt so many needy souls and take care of those that aren't your responsibility, but do so out of love. That is admirable. You don't receive any monetary gain from what you do; yet, you still do it.

You pick up where others have dropped the ball, and you are making a difference in so many lives. They are blessed to have you.

You have been autonomous, for the most part, since you were sixteen. You've been on your own by and large.

You graduated high school, enrolled in college, and lived completely on your own without any money from the state. Wish more Americans were like you! Kudos to you, girlfriend. Kudos to you.

You've suffered a most tragic loss, and you have become a better human being because of it. I know the pain of his absence must ache inside you, but if we look at things from above, he is with you and he will always be there. His loss thrust you into a new phase of your life where you are thriving.

You grew up quickly, before you should have, and you should be so proud of how you handled it. I know I am. You have risen above his loss in the physical world like a champion. In the words of Ralph Waldo Emerson, "We acquire the strength we have overcome."

Continue to make me proud, Emmy, and look out world.... this young lady is fierce.

In closing, keep that gorgeous smile of yours beaming and continue to brighten the days of those around you.

You are LIGHT, Emmy. You seriously glow and those around you want to be in your beautiful presence. You brighten any room, and our time together I sincerely cherish.

I love you.

Ro

# 15

To my beloved students,

While formulating this final group message to you all, I am smiling, overwhelmed with pride. The courage that it took to confide in me about your pain is admirable. Sharing it with the world is downright brave. I'm grateful that you were placed in my life. Spirit made it happen and as a result, we have created a book together.

You are all such strong human beings, and sharing your very private details of a most difficult time in your life speaks to the types of people that you are. You are hurting, yet in spite of some of the atrocities you've experienced, you forgive.

Mahatma Gandhi said, "The weak can never forgive. Forgiveness is the attribute of the strong."

I agree.

Forgiveness is a theme in each of your stories. You forgive the deceased parent, your living parent, your family members, and your God.

> "To forgive is to set a prisoner free and discover that
> the prisoner was you." -Lewis B. Smedes

Please continue to forgive yourself as well. There is nothing you could have done to change or alter the outcome of your loved one's death. Nothing. It was destiny——Maktub.

Some people doubt your generation, but knowing each of you, I'm not worried. You've come a long way from what you've endured and that gives me great hope for you and the future of our world. You could have easily taken destructive roads based on your early traumas, but you have done quite the opposite. You are living good, honest lives with promising futures.

Thank you for stepping up and helping others like yourselves. Your stories are raw and painful, and what a difference your insight will have on other teens! Whether you realize it or not, each and every one of you has impacted my life, and I am a better human being for having known you.

I'd like to close with a quote from Mother Teresa, "We cannot all do great things. But we can do small things with great love."

That you did, my special ones!

Much love to you always and only the best,

Ms. Romero

They that love beyond the world cannot be separated by it.
Death cannot kill what never dies.

-William Penn

# 16

## FOR THE PARENTS READING THIS BOOK

MY STUDENTS SHARED their personal stories of loss with intention. They want your children to know that they are not alone in their grief, that many others their age have gone through difficult and trying times. Their intention is for your child to find peace.

Several of my students' losses are still very fresh and many need to find a counselor they connect with to help them work through their trauma. I hope this book helps not only your child, but also you. I hope that you seek outside help if your child needs it, and that you are instrumental in turning a deeply painful situation into a livable one. If you are willing, there is great hope.

Below is a list of points that I have found to be healing for young people experiencing the loss of a loved one.

### YOUR CHILD NEEDS SOMEONE TO TALK TO

Your child needs a support person to talk with about what has happened. It could be his or her favorite teacher (past or present), a good school counselor, a licensed therapist, a living parent, someone at your place of worship or through a hospice support group, or family members who are open to truly hearing your child and who can help them without them even knowing that they're being helped. Good listeners are essential.

The key element necessary is that your child CONNECTS with their support person. If there is no connection, little if any help will come from it. They won't open themselves up to share freely and this will hinder the healing process.

Shortly before my mother died, she asked me to go see a counselor. I had never been to a counselor before and wasn't too keen on the idea, but I couldn't deny my dying mother. She wanted me to schedule at least three visits so I could talk about all the emotions I was experiencing. Somewhat reluctantly, I scheduled my three sessions. The counselor appointed by my insurance company wasn't the right fit for me. I didn't feel comfortable, and as a result, I wasn't completely honest with her. I didn't let her in to the depths of my emotions, and consequently, it wasn't particularly helpful.

That said, I believe it is of utmost importance that you set up at least three sessions with a counselor who is the right fit for your child. Search for the counselor or support group that your child can trust and confide in. It will make the healing process more natural and productive.

If you feel that the counselor makes your child uncomfortable, move on. Don't worry about the feelings of the counselor. It's about what's best for your child. Make sure, in whatever route you take, that they are engaged in helping your child. There are many good counselors who truly care about their clients. Find them.

On a flip side, books and/or audio books can also be a great source of comfort for a teen that is reluctant to respond to therapy or one who refuses to attend. A list of resources is provided at the end of this book, and it is a great place to start.

⸺

## YOUR CHILD NEEDS TIME TO GRIEVE

"Grief is not a disorder, a disease or a sign of weakness. It is an emotional, physical and spiritual necessity, the price you pay for love. The only cure for grief is to grieve."

- Earl Grollman

Grieving is a process that takes time. Suggest your child keep a journal of his or her emotions and feelings surrounding the death as well as a place to record his or her memories of the deceased loved one. A written document serves as a good reminder of where they've been and how far they've come. We sometimes forget how truly awful something we've endured was until we revisit it in our own words. It can be very cathartic to see our growth.

I noted that many of my students felt release and relief from participating in this book through sharing their stories. I observed changes in them while they simply remembered the loved one and acknowledged the pain of their loss. A detectable transformation occurred from their participation in this writing process. It happened for them, and it can also happen for your child.

Waiting, however, to heal and deal with these deep emotions can have consequences. I've included excerpts of a story written by a friend of mine from junior high who lost her father to suicide during our 8th grade year. I remember when it occurred and how awkward the situation was for those who knew her. What do you say to a classmate in that situation? How does one behave around her? Shannon writes about her loss nearly thirty years later for the purpose of this book. I believe her words show how over time we heal, but they also validate the importance of early intervention in the grieving process. Here is what she says:

"Losing my father at the age of 14 was devastating. As I sit here and write this, I cry. I still cry about losing him, and I'm 45 years old. Losing a parent as a child is heart breaking and something we will grieve for many, many years.

The day I found out that I had lost my father, the coroner showed up at our house and told us there had been a car accident. I could tell by the look on their faces that my father was dead. I was fourteen when my dad took his own life.

The police eventually found his car. He had driven off a cliff on a canyon road on the way to the beach. Apparently there were marks on the road that informed the police that he had "punched it" over the cliff, confirming that it was suicide.

I did not really start to grieve my father's death until I moved away to college. At that time, I began to dream about him quite frequently. In these dreams I would see him at public places like malls and airports. Often he would be on his bike. This made me very happy. But then I would wake up and realize it was a dream.

I believe when you lose a parent to suicide, anger is something that you frequently come back to. I wish I had been more open to therapy. I was a hard-headed teenager, and I didn't think that I needed any help. I was very angry and took it out on my mom, which I regret.

If you are going through the loss or have lost your parent I encourage you to seek others out that have gone through the loss of a parent so you can talk about your loss or impending loss with people that love you. Stay connected to friends and family. Be grateful for what you do have and show gratitude daily. Focus on the good in your life. Figure out a way to give back to society and help others that have gone through what you have. I feel gratitude and giving back is the key to a happy and healthy life."

As Shannon confided, she wasn't open to therapy and referred to herself as a hard-headed teenager who didn't start grieving until college. Her resentment and anger may have been lessened had she worked through it when her loss was fresh.

Today Shannon is a veteran high school counselor who also strongly suggests that your child find a trustworthy person that he or she connects with to talk about his or her feelings of loss and how to heal.

Young people may not think it is necessary at the moment, but hindsight is 20/20. My philosophy is that talking about your loss won't kill you, so why not? All you stand to lose is time.

—※—

## CREATING RITUALS

Please do not bury and ignore the loss of the loved one. Some of you might not want to bring up the past in fear that you may hurt your child further by rehashing it, but your child needs a means of expression and to keep the memory of their lost loved one alive until he or she moves on in a natural way.

"Death ends a life, not a relationship." ~Mitch Albom, *Tuesdays With Morrie*

Many of my students were never spoken to about the parent or loved one that died. The topic was avoided so as to not upset the child and possibly the grieving parent. My student Oras never spoke about his father's crossing until this book project. It wasn't until I inquired and listened to him tell his story that he shed many tears and started to smile about his father and remember the good times he shared with his dad. Our dialogue was a blessing, and I literally witnessed him healing right before my eyes.

Silence and ignoring the death is a mistake for the child still grieving. It will have a greater long-term negative effect if you avoid the topic because eventually it's going to come up in conversation, and it will be awkward and uncomfortable for the child. As an alternative, I recommend creating a ritual or celebration around the lost loved one.

ON THEIR BIRTHDAY

My daughter and I write letters to my mother on helium balloons every year on her birthday and release them into the sky. Our letters are long and shed many layers of our current life, trials, and tribulations. I make her favorite strawberry jello dessert, and we enjoy it as we dedicate our time to her.

ON HOLIDAYS

My family toasts our deceased loved ones every holiday dinner. Our large extended Mexican family does a shot of Tequila for them every year. It's a tradition that occurs the same time every Thanksgiving and Christmas for willing participants of drinking age. I look forward to these times when our loved ones are recognized, honored, and celebrated. Our family bond is undeniable. When one is no longer with us, they still remain important. They are family and always will be. No one is forgotten.

"To live in hearts we leave behind is not to die."
— Thomas Campbell

ON THE ANNIVERSARY OF THEIR DEATH

My daughter and I recognize the day my mom left us here on Earth as the day she took up a new position "upstairs" full time as an angel. We view my mother as a guardian angel watching over us from above. To recognize her passing we may eat at her favorite restaurant or watch her favorite movie. We do something that she enjoyed doing. Again, it is a time to celebrate the woman who brought me into this world, who loved me dearly, and who is still a part of my life. By honoring my mother in this fashion, I stay connected, and I'm happy.

## HONOR THE LOSS OF A PARENT

When a parent dies, a void is born. Holidays such as Mother's Days and Father's Days are tough ones to endure, especially for children.

In school, art projects creating gifts and cards for the parent are routine. Unfortunately, some kids don't have a parent to make a gift or card for. If this is the situation for your child, you can teach your child to go ahead and make their card or gift placing it next to the parent's picture as a show of devotion. Honoring the loss of a parent takes the sting out of many holidays and brings peace. Parents, please help facilitate this for your children.

---

## SOMETHING TO THINK ABOUT

"If you have a sister and she dies,
do you stop saying you have one?
Or are you always a sister,
even when the other half of the equation is gone?"

— Jodi Picoult, *My Sister's Keeper*

Of course. You will always be his or her sister, brother, son, daughter, cousin, or friend—even when the other half of the equation dies. LOVE is forever.

"When we can hear or see or sense
our deceased loved ones directly,
then we know we are separated
only in a temporary way."

—Dr. Brian Weiss

Be open to this. Share this. It will COMPLETELY change your experience with grief. Accept that the soul of the departed loved one is with us always, feels the love that we have for them, and will be there for us when we die. We will all experience grief eventually and how we react and cope can and will determine our experience. As hard as death may seem to accept, unfortunately it is a reality. Even though our loved one is gone in body, they certainly don't need to be gone from our hearts and our thoughts.

---

## GIVE YOUR CHILD A FRAMED PHOTOGRAPH

As for a final suggestion, frame a picture of your child and their lost loved one in their bedroom. It's a way of honoring them and a reminder of how blessed we were to have had them in our life. I recommend that it's a picture of the two of them together if possible. The following story explains my recommendation.

One of my writers was a very troubled boy with a bleak future who was being raised by his grandpa. For a class timeline assignment, he informed me that he had no pictures of his mother or father in his house.

After the assignment due date and seeing the cool presentation boards turned in by his fellow classmates, he brought me a picture of him with his mother that he found buried in some hidden photo album. The picture made me smile because you could see the joy in his mother's eyes and feel the love exchanged between the two.

He accidently left the photo in my classroom—no surprise there. He is a junior high boy. So I took the opportunity to have his picture framed for him. When I returned it to him in the beautiful frame, he lit up. He was so surprised, and he absolutely loved it.

He tells me that the picture frame is on his nightstand, and he says, "Good Morning, Mom," and "Good night, Mom," every day to her.

Before the frame, my student simply existed without a mother figure in his life. He was not acknowledging the woman that brought him into the world and whom he loved so dearly. He hadn't actually seen how much she adored him until he found the photo. The picture didn't lie. She adored her baby boy, and the framed photo is a reminder to him of the LOVE they shared, and it has brought him much peace.

This student in question has since turned his life around and wants to live his life for his mother who died much too young. The framed picture is also a reminder of that quest.

Since she lived such a short life, he has shared that he is going to live his life as she would have wanted and the best one imaginable. He has since given me his portal code for his high school grades so I can check online and see all his success in school. I'm happy to report that he is passing all his classes and is on track for graduating high school! I am so, so, proud of him! What a difference bringing his mom back into his life has made!

---

## THERE IS HOPE

Healing can and will occur with time for those that are willing. Recovery takes time and everyone will heal at his or her own pace. I cannot stress enough "for those that are willing." It's essential that your child is an active participant, and it's my opinion that it starts with this:

"It's not forgetting that heals. It's remembering."
— Amy Greene, *Bloodroot*

Remember, honor, and heal.

Parents, tread lightly—listen clearly—love deeply—and most importantly, allow them to grieve.

This poem is the perfect closer to this book:

"Speak Their Name"

Someone I love has gone away
And life is not the same
The greatest gift that you can give
Is just to speak their name.

I need to hear the stories
And the tales of days gone past
I need for you to understand
These memories must last.

We cannot make more memories
Since they're no longer here
So when you speak of them to me
It's music to my ear.

~Kelly Polley Giesler, Out of the Ashes

# LIST OF RESOURCES

**Amazing poetry** about overcoming loss:
*On facebook:* www.facebook.com/outoftheasheswerise7
*Website:* outoftheashes007.wix.com/photo-memorial-by-kp

**Novels:**
*Tiger Eyes* by Judy Blume (girl deals w/murder of father)

*Beat the Turtle Drum* by C. Greene (loss of sibling)

**Self Help books:**
*Talking to Heaven* by James Van Praagh

*Straight Talk About Death for Teenagers: How to Cope with Losing Someone You Love* by Earl A. Grollman

*After Suicide: Living with the Questions* by Eileen Kuehn

**Movies:**
An EXCELLENT link for movies categorized by need and/or loss:
http://www.selfhealingexpressions.com/grief_movies.shtml

# ABOUT THE AUTHOR

SUSAN ROMERO IS an award-winning teacher with over two decades of middle school experience. She studied at San Diego State University in the School of Education and earned a Master's Degree in Educational Administration at Cal Lutheran University. Passionate about counseling, she mentors children and teens through life's trials and tribulations focusing on increasing self-esteem and creating self-love. She has an innate ability to help young people cope with and heal from loss. Susan's second book, *What I Couldn't Teach You in the Classroom*, is coming in 2015. She resides in Riverbank, California, with her daughter Jordan and her two beloved canines Lacy Marie and Mandy Marie.

C.Lit BF 723 .G75 R67 2014
Romero, Susan,
Teens dealing with death

35016255R00093

Made in the USA
San Bernardino, CA
06 May 2019